Meeting God

Meeting God

RICKY SARPONG

This is a work of fiction. Names, characters, places, and incidents either are the product of the author's imagination or are used fictitiously. Any resemblance to actual persons, living or dead, events, or locales is entirely coincidental.

Copyright © 2022 by Ricky Sarpong

All rights reserved. No part of this book may be reproduced or used in any manner without written permission of the copyright owner except for the use of quotations in a book review.

First edition 2022

Book design by Publishing Push

ISBN 978-1-80227-422-6 (paperback)
ISBN 978-1-80227-421-9 (ebook)

Published by PublishingPush.com

Typeset using Atomik ePublisher from Easypress Technologies

This book is dedicated to Agnes Boateng, my mum.

Introduction

Over the years, but more so in recent times, there have been some notable disappointments with the conduct and character of the Church. Many feel let down by both leadership and laity. This has not helped in addressing the doubts and reservations of many about the existence of God and even the integrity of the Christian movement. Reports of abuse and despicable actions by clergy and laity have forced many to the choice of moving away from what they represent. This book seeks to consider the fairness of such actions by examining the dynamics at play. You can't fairly label a group by just meeting a few. How is it unprejudiced to call a person a Christian just by seeing them walk from a church building with a Bible in hand? That is no less than calling anything that comes out of a garage a car. This book is about meeting the one behind the Church and its faith: God. It is about determining the reality and nature of such a meeting. The point is to bring home the need for a meeting with God or Christ in a personal way.

    The chapters of this book don't scream the subject of faith or belief at you, but help guide anyone to an experience which is worth having. Yes, there is every known talk about the Church, Christ and God but they are more the experiences and reality of others. The question is: can you make them yours? Would that make any difference? If you knew about the story of the blind men who tried to share their experience after meeting an elephant, as shared in this book, you would realise the nature and complexity of personal encounters. You would understand the essence and need for meeting the God or Christ of the Church and not just the Church of God or Christ. Personal encounters offer a subjective take which could be fitting and suitable for the self. It offers a reality that others may only wonder about and a solid bridge between belief and realism. A meeting with God would put any subsequent meetings with the Church in their appropriate light and you will realise this within the succeeding chapters.

One major point considered in this book is the matter of the Church as a "work in progress". This suggests the existence of temporary and permanent elements in the midst of it. Any talk or consideration of these elements therefore must be in their proper perspectives. We can't have one bad apple serve as the determinant for the quality or character of an entire harvest. Jesus, who is God's Son or simply God, had a thief and a betrayer in the midst of his disciples. In fact, he picked him since he chose all. Do we get to use that alone to determine the quality of his choices or the integrity of his leadership and witness?

This book is meant to start conversations and self-reflections, which you will find at the end of every chapter. It skims philosophical and scientific thoughts, and aims to expose truths that are mostly traded-off for convenience and traditions. It will help you to meet God if you haven't already and determine if you truly have. For the one who has doubts and misgivings about the whole subject matter, be encouraged to give this book a read without any preconceptions and you could end up with an encounter. God calls all to come. Let's take Him up on His invitation. I pray that you meet Him!

Chapter 1

Meeting! What is it?

Before we go on about meeting God, let us consider what makes a meeting. It has been determined over the years that the human community thrives on the premise of interrelations. In fact, many people do sometimes aspire to be "islands" but that is never realised because it is not truly palpable. Humans are social beings that function effectively and productively in social settings and systems. The situation of man living and dwelling alone was seen by his creator, God, as "not good" (Genesis 2:18), and admittedly anything deemed not good by God can never be anything else. In social settings, people tend to meet other people to form relationships. Meetings serve in making friends, lifetime partners, couples and even enemies. I have met many people in my life and one that still holds my interest and heart is my wife. Some of your lifetime friends are people you met in school, a park, during an incident or event. There are people you met while meeting other people. Meetings do, in essence, affect destinies. There are some dynamics to the act of meeting which we need to explore.

The Meaning

In its simplest definition, "to meet" is to come into contact with another, a coming together especially at a particular time or place. The Merriam-Webster dictionary offers a helpful definition which is "to come into the presence of". This meaning alludes to the idea of immediacy and closeness. To meet is, as said, to primarily come into contact with an animate thing or person. You are right to meet a neighbour's cat rather than their table. True meetings which can be deemed as encounters are essentially founded on engagements or stimulations. The experience is relatively personal, affective and is best explained by the parties involved.

There have been times when some meetings have been cast in unrealistic renderings. You cannot claim to have met a celebrity when it was on the person's social media account. Neither can you claim to have met someone who actually got introduced to you in a story. Such situations have generated wrong impressions and facilitated irreconcilable actions. I once witnessed such a remarkable case at an event. I was with a group of gentlemen at said event who had separated from the main crowd for a chat. We were suddenly approached by another man who was casting insinuations about a member of the group while repeatedly asking for the whereabouts of the victim. His actions were unnerving and disturbing particularly because the gentleman he was verbally abusing was right before him. I felt he was either bold or just hopelessly misguided. Perceiving his possible ignorance, one member of the group asked him if he knew the gentleman in question, to which he replied, "I hear he is here somewhere", all the time looking around but beyond the group. Finally, the victim introduced himself to the guy to the latter's horror and shame. I had never seen before then such an awkward situation like that.

I have met people claiming to meet people they have never met. Maybe you have too. The thought of it can make you wonder sometimes but there is a basis to it. This brings up the matter of the two known forms of meeting people. There is the direct form of meeting which is typically face-to-face or the popular kind which simply requires one to be in the presence of the one being met. That is the purest and most realistic form of meeting which has birthed many relationships and experiences. What is captured or drawn from such kind of meetings can only be couched in personal thoughts and sentiments. The registered experience is first-hand and can never be tampered or doctored. Anytime we have the opportunity to meet, if we haven't already, it will be that kind of meeting and I genuinely look forward to it.

The other form of meeting is the indirect kind, and it is pretty common today with the help of current technology. Indirect meetings are fictive, mostly distant, and mediated. In the immediate past, we got to meet several people through the print media. We read their thoughts, shared their dreams, and sighted their fears. Most of such experiences were muted or veiled. This was when you got to meet someone before meeting the person. In many cases, you had to make up a face and even a personality before maybe one day finally being in the presence of it. Technology today has advanced and enhanced, in some ways, this phenomenon. Now, there are cases where you can put a face to a story without a direct meeting and other instances where the entire face could be a borrowed or "invented" one. The available media platforms of the twenty-first century are facilitating an augmented reality which is undermining the core elements of truth and integrity. Reality is being falsified in real ways now where make-believes are presently being made to be believed. I recently received a text message from a colleague pastor which can be cited as an example in this case. This pastor was clearly troubled, if not horrified, by a video he had seen making rounds on social media. Said video showed a pastor claiming to exorcise demonic spirits from congregants by supposedly shaving their private parts publicly, though victims were not entirely exposed in the shots. It was obvious this friend had his judgement cap on and his supposition machinery firing on all cylinders since the pastor in the video was of my nationality, and it had been a while since I was last contacted by this friend. You can make the association yourself. It was good that he did this anyway because I had the chance to explain to him that it was a ruse and, in fact, a skit portraying certain prevailing ills. I don't think he believed me given the nature of the video, but he did come back a couple of days later with another video shot by another pastor to explain as I did. Well, I felt relieved that my views had been vindicated by another, but the incident left me with a very bad taste in my mouth. Apparently, this was a second skit of a similar timbre put out there by this actor (pastor). What happened to a disclaimer? What happened to giving unsuspecting audiences a note of warning or intention? What was a person to make of pastors if this happened to be the first one they had the chance to meet? This is what is currently defining meetings – an augmented reality. Situations where experiences are made or deemed real when they never are, and this is only the beginning.

Some More Complexities

Besides the above referenced difficulties with indirect forms of meeting, there are further complexities with the entire subject of meeting. For now, we know the two basic kinds but there are also two methods worth citing. The first method is the normal planned meeting. This is consistent with a prearranged meeting and offers a measure of experience which is either as expected or a let-down. Most planned meetings are heavily dictated by known variables, gathered information or facts which tend to set an expectation or paint a picture. In planned meetings, parties happen to have a fair estimation of what to expect. You don't plan to meet a pastor only to meet with a psychoanalyst. Such an experience may be surprising and definitely groundless. So, planned meetings hardly guesstimate surprises given the knowledge already acquired about a subject or party in a meeting. Here is where we get to have further complexities.

Knowledge, mostly acquired through media sources, electronic, print or even the age-old word of mouth, has the tendency and potency to often shape our views and perceptions leaving us with some biases and presuppositions. No one truly walks around with a mind of their own. We get influenced immeasurably by the information we gather every day. We know, for instance, that no child is born racist but may become one over time given environmental and social influences. This complexity creates a situation where experiences gained from planned meetings are gravely managed. When we have bad information on a subject, expectations of a meeting are predetermined to be bad, whereas good information conditions us for a worthwhile experience. At times, even when a meeting which was presupposed to be a good one turns out not as expected, we find for it a reasonable excuse, at least to ourselves. We never believe the experience because we had in mind what to expect and still look for it. In converse situations, we see the gravity of the anomaly. When you expect to have a terrible meeting with someone you gathered was terrible but happened to have a remarkable one, you unconsciously try to find that incredulous and would even work at making that the case. Planned meetings with biases manage experiences and this, as a complexity, will be closely looked at later.

The other method of meeting we need to look at is chance meetings.

These are simply meetings which are never planned for. One typical feature of a chance meeting is the suddenness making it bereft of any preconceived expectations and notions. The experience is therefore not managed but can either be momentous or insignificant. A meeting that makes significant impact would require some foreknowledge of the subject. If the Prime Minister of Ireland should find himself on a holiday resort somewhere in Africa, the possible response to saying to someone he meets there, "Hi, I am the Taoiseach of Ireland" would be, "What? Who do you say you are?" The extent of the void in recognition can only be imagined and the possible disinterest in a meeting like that may follow. However, should the same person perhaps have a relative resident in Ireland or be knowledgeable about some facts of the country, the response would be different. The meeting would offer a better experience for both parties barring any existing preconceptions. Chance meetings are therefore mostly meaningful when there is some prior knowledge but are better nonetheless for unmanaged experiences. The point is that someone coming from a remote village in the Amazon will be perplexed to see me excited about meeting with the President of the United States while standing by me. Whilst he will have nothing to see nor experience, I can't help but have it all. So prior knowledge is good to have before a meeting but the same tend to manage experiences.

Managed Experiences

Meeting God is like meeting any other person or entity and understanding the various dynamics helps to put things into perspective. As previously discussed, a meeting can be direct or indirect, planned or by chance, and weighing in on the experience matters. The fullest benefits to a meeting can be secured once expectations are properly managed. Life as we see it is an artful work of deft balancing and managing. Scales get easily tipped. A good thing can well become a bad thing with ease. Managing experiences is a complexity which needs to be tactfully gauged and carefully exercised. A trip to a paradise island cannot just be fully appraised by the dazzling pictures in a brochure. The pictures are well and good, but they don't tell the whole or true story, as a personal experience would do.

Over the years, some psychologists have spent time exploring the subject of contact, or in our case, meetings, and have made some remarkable determinations. They have discovered our group affiliations or associations do inform our default settings for attitudes and beliefs which affect how we make contact. This phenomenon essentially dictates the results of intergroup contact. What groups tend to know about each other ultimately affects how they interact. In fact, the fullest potential of a contact or meeting is realised when meeting parties, firstly, commit to meet and secondly, do so with their biases inhibited. According to Gordon Allport (contact theorist), such contact, especially between two different groups, actually promotes acceptance and tolerance. This is managing experiences. In effect, your experience in a meeting is extensively helped if your information about the other party doesn't predispose you unnecessarily, unfairly, and completely. Information content, agents of dispensation and manner of delivery are therefore paramount in influencing the outcome of meetings and so must be carefully managed. So, know but be judicious about what you know before a meeting or contact. Should it, however, be the case that you have no prior knowledge before a meeting, then it becomes incumbent that you avoid a lethargic attitude and impassivity. So, you can meet God without knowing whom you are meeting but it helps if you do. However, just having an open mind about His meeting will help with the experience.

Reflection

1. *Assess now*: Have you ever questioned the relevance of connecting or associating with people? Have you been deterred from seeking further associations due to negative experiences? How well have you done in managing experiences? Would you agree that you have had biases which affected the outcome of some meetings you've had? Do you research information shared with you?
2. *Consider now*: I guess thoughts of being an "island" isolated from communities and family have come to mind at some point but do well to discard them. You need to connect; you need to meet people. It is never good to be alone. The best you can do is to develop circles of

friends or associates. Friends or companions who can provide finance cannot necessarily be compassionate when needed. Friends graced to counsel may not be suited for business partnership. Jesus had three known circles of associates (disciples). There were the three (Mark 9:2), the twelve (Matthew 10:1-4), and the seventy-two (Luke 10:1). Make the effort to manage your meeting experiences by managing your biases and this you can do by managing information gathered or received beforehand. Don't underestimated the influence and effect of bad information. Never treat second-hand information as first-hand material. It is always best to know things for yourself.

Chapter 2

I Once Met a King

I had an earlier career in journalism and radio broadcasting. It was a career I had for a considerable period with its accompanying experiences. My numerous yet exciting activities brought me in contact with many people of diverse positions and backgrounds. I had meetings with prominent politicians, as well as religious, community and opinion leaders. The inherit demand of objectivity in the conduct of my work helped offset any notions of prejudice and presuppositions. To be honest, despite managed expectations, no meetings were typically approached without any premise or hunches. In effect, there was always the impression of "a meeting before a meeting". At one point in my career, over twenty years ago, I had the privilege of managing a radio station in a region in Ghana which serves as the seat of a prominent monarch. This king has far-reaching influence and a historically notable affair with the British Empire. The king of the Asantes is one you hardly get to meet yet I got the chance to meet him.

The Hype – The Meeting Before the Meeting

As previously mentioned, there is no denying the notion of always having a form of a meeting before any meeting. It may come in the nature of information gathered, stories read or heard, pictures seen or everyday banter. Before getting the unique chance of meeting the king of the Ashanti kingdom, I had come to meet him in the pages of the national newspapers, the numerous electronic media platforms and through awe-inducing stories. The Ashanti king comes from a long lineage of kings that serve as monarchs of an empire which dates back to the seventeenth century. This empire particularly came into prominence, and in the eyes of the world, as it resisted the colonial exploits of the British in the then Gold Coast, now Ghana. Its stories are awash with heroism, uncanny bravery, and feats. One unusual but fantastic story is that of the golden stool. Historical facts indicate that, at the founding stages of the empire, the chief priest or spiritual guide of the people conjured from the heavens a golden stool that landed in the lap of the first king marking him then as the chosen leader of the clans that had agreed to unite to form the empire. The golden stool is purported to be the unifying totem of the Asantes and its presence in the kingdom ensures its unity and continuity. The current king that I had the chance to meet happens to be named after the founding king, Osei Tutu.

The present king is not without his fabulous stories. People who have attended his sessions of adjudication in his palatial courts have attributed to him a remarkable gift of wisdom, most affably comparing him to the legendary King Solomon. His efforts at modernising the monarchy in order to make it relevant in the present century has not hurt nor impaired the traditional institutions; institutions which are rich in culture and heritage. There is still presence in his rule; a sense of sovereignty and invincibility. He is deemed one with no equals, one to judge but never to be judged, a custodian of all that is good, fair, and just. This is the kind of hype that you can hardly ignore or avoid being impressed by before a meeting. A meeting with the Ashanti king summarily invokes a sense of meeting with a king from one of the Old Testament narratives.

The Meeting

The meeting with the Ashanti king was arranged many weeks before the set date by one hardworking member of our radio news team who was our assignee on the palace's media outfit. The day arrived with its obvious feeling of excitement. The team was led by the chief executive of our radio organisation, and I went along as the general manager. We arrived on time and got invited into one of the king's courts promptly. There was a lot to take in inside the guest court and much more to get you distracted. My quick attempt at a panoptic view of the court was cut short by the sudden call to attention by one of the linguists of the king. I did, however, get to savour the rich images and artefacts of the distinctive Ashanti tradition displayed around the rather small space of the court. The atmosphere was more than I expected. It was striking and a bit overwhelming. My mind was racing just trying to internalise the sights and sounds being captured with the occasional voice of the king's linguist coming through. There were several officials of the court present with a few being the king's linguists. According to the set protocols of the palace and kingdom, the king never gets to speak directly to anyone officially. He speaks through his linguist and his audience communicates with him in the same way.

The linguist who had called us to attention did so to lay down the expected nature and conduct of the meeting. He clearly explained what we were expected to do when the king entered to give us audience, who could approach him for a handshake and the fact we needed to delegate a member of our group to speak on our behalf. The instructions were quite firm and incontestable, and like the commandments of God to Israel, they were to ensure a fruitful meeting and experience. Some of us nodded in agreement while others were simply irresponsive, still awe-struck by the occasion. I was having a memorable moment and was registering every second of it. Then it happened.

There was a sudden hush that fell on the room and a swift yet coordinated move of all present to stand. I turned in the direction of the king's seat and he was there. Yes, he was there. I might have missed him come in or he just had a way of appearing, but he was there. It may be a bit stretched or even exaggerated to suggest that the king's coming, and presence, had a sense of otherworldliness about it. That notwithstanding, he clearly made an impression. He came into the room and invoked a measure of silence that could make anyone hear the sound of a watch tick. His linguist introduced us to him and proceeded to enquire about the reason for our presence in the king's court. All responses were to the linguist, a kind of Moses, and never to the king. So, we indicated through our spokesperson our cause to pay our respects, offer our gifts and to announce the presence of our organisation in his kingdom. We were heartily received by him and were offered his support and counsel. Such was the meeting, brief yet with enough memories and lessons to last a lifetime.

My Impressions

The clearest effects of our experiences are the impressions made. Such impressions are typically influenced by expectations. Either you have your impressions of an experience conform to, exceed or fall short of what you expected. In some instances, as previously cited, an experience can produce some measurable effect without prior expectations. I had some expectations when going in to meet with the Ashanti king and they were met and even exceeded. The expected flamboyance was the only thing missing. The court's set up was unique yet simple while still bearing the air of awesomeness and clout. My impressions were what I call direct and indirect. The direct impressions were drawn from the physical and tangible experience of the meeting while indirect impressions were the lessons gathered from the meeting which shall be my focus here.

Meeting With Sovereignty and Not a Personality – One can easily point out that the king of the Asantes is a mere man or mortal, but is he? In fact, he is known to be a proficient golf player and has friends he plays with. He has a wife and family yet, in his capacity as the king, his sovereignty comes to play and never his personality. Meeting with him as a king is meeting with the power, authority, charge and graces of his kingdom. An act against him is an act against his seat of power. Stepping into his presence is essentially stepping before his rule and the scope and depth of his government. I learnt in our meeting why and how to appreciate such occasions and cherish them. When you meet with anyone, you tend to also meet with all that makes or comes with them. That explained the character and nature of the atmosphere the king's presence generated during the meeting. We were meeting with a kingdom and not just a king.

Mediated Meetings – There are some meetings which are mediated and that with a king, or any such authority, is an example. Meetings of such nature which are held in court are also before other officials and not without formalities. Pleasantries are mostly limited or barred, making any personal interactions a remote expectation or occurrence. So, you never get to chitchat with the Ashanti king in court, just like the people of Israel never got to have personal meetings with God. I learnt then that to have any authority, like a king, get personal with you was honourable and an opportunity to be relished and adored.

Not Meeting a King Empty-Handed – Our meeting with the king necessitated us showing up with a gift. It was an honour and a real pleasure seeing him accept it. I learnt that is the norm and not an act just carried out under advisement. The similarity with the Old Testament's command of God to Israel is rather striking: "Three times a year all your men must appear before the Lord your God at the place he will choose: at the Festival of Unleavened Bread, the Festival of Weeks, and the Festival of Tabernacles. **No one should appear before the Lord empty-handed**: Each of you must bring a gift in proportion to the way the Lord your God has blessed you." (Deuteronomy 16: 16-17 NIV, emphasis mine)

I can only admit that my meeting with the Ashanti king put some matters involving meeting with God into perspective and helped shape my understanding and thoughts, which I share in this book. The prominent point though is the unique, vivid, and personal experience of the meeting which can never be fictionised and will remain with me. It was my experience. My meeting with the king.

Reflection

1. *Assess now*: Have you had any encounters with persons of authority? Did you have any expectations before the meeting and did that affect the experience? Have you ever given a thought to the power and scope of command of the person of authority you met? Was the meeting mediated or personal? If personal, did it feel special?

2. *Consider now*: Meeting with a person of power is not a meeting with an individual or personality, it is a meeting with something more. The contact should be measured not by limited perspectives or parameters but by the scope of the authority. What may be known of

a king in his personal circumstances might not be the same as what is known of his dominance and control. A meeting with such should not be clouded by personal judgements but its humbling effects must be fully allowed and appreciated. In this way, should a meeting with a person of authority be conducted in a more personal and intimate way, it must be deemed an honour and valued as such. An abuse of such privilege is a slighting of an office, seat, or power. When you consider every person to be of authority given the unique charge, particular domain or authority exercised, be it at home, business, or vocation, then there is some mystery to every meeting and an appropriate conduct to each one.

Chapter 3

Meeting God

The subject of God is a dicey one and has, over the years, drawn close attention in different quarters. There are complexities which we need not explore here. What prevails is the simple question – is there a God or not? The point of meeting Him then becomes secondary. The most obvious conviction in empirical terms is that God cannot be believed or proven to exist. For many who hold such convictions, the reasoning and parameters for such determination is moulded by unanswered questions and many unknown variables presently beyond our scope of understanding. Honestly, to live in a world of proofs is to live in a world of limited reality. The fact I have no TV set to show to a village dweller in a remote location on the planet does not suggest that my belief, experience, and knowledge of one is void and his unbelief valid. Not knowing the existence of a thing does not pragmatically confirm its nihility. Besides, any attempt at figuring out a thing is relatively dependent on the scope and measure of it. How long do you think it would take an ant to figure out every aspect of an elephant in its study of it? At any point, while studying its head, would it be appropriate or right for it to suggest that it has no tail? Wouldn't it be hasty or possibly unseemly for anyone to suppose that there is no God based on our limited knowledge of Him?

When we consider the depth, scope, and mystery of the universe, it is of little wonder that we have such contestation of its creator. The universe is estimated to have come into being over 13.8 billion years ago, perhaps part of a multi-universe, populated with billions of galaxies which have billions of stars and systems of planets, of which ours is one. Efforts at determining the origins of all things have not missed that of the universe. How did the universe come to be and was someone or something behind its formation? People of the Abrahamic religious traditions or influence will say God created it all while persons of the scientific community allude to a "big bang theory". While the scientific community appears to have their case supposedly clarified by their theory, and that of evolution, it still begs more questions than that of the religious position. There is always the "chicken or egg" question, and the infinite regression conundrum. What was before? What was before what was before, and so on until the beginning? What caused that which caused the end we see, and so on and so on? The much-celebrated Christian theologian, Thomas Aquinas, proposed five views in response to this puzzle which essentially proves the existence of God. He explained God as the Unmoved Mover who first moved all things, the First Cause that initiated all causes, the Necessary Being whose non-existence is an impossibility and from whom the existence of all contingent beings is ultimately derived, the Absolute Being: the highest form of all things true, pure, good, noble and the like, and the Grand Designer. This is the God of the Abrahamic religious traditions.

In the first book of the Holy Scriptures for both Jews and Christians, which is the Old Testament, there is the simplest and clearest revelation of the origin of the universe: "In the beginning God created the heavens and the earth." (Genesis 1:1). Here, in this statement, is an audacious declaration of truth. The universe – the heavens and the earth – is seen to have God as the creator. You reflect on that, and you can draw some reasonable and judicious meanings and conclusions. For instance, if all was created then there should be purpose to all things. Like man-made products, all created things cannot be without defined scope and limits of functionality. One cannot use a hairdryer to boil water, just as we can't have the sea waves not return to sea at some point from the beach. Such considerations suggest accountability and responsibility and who bears them other than the creator. Besides, there is much known now about the universe to suggest a reasonable design to it. The set location of the earth in the solar system known as the Goldilocks' region (habitable zone around a star) is a case in point. How easy and tactical can it be for the earth to find itself in the "just right" position from the sun to support life? Which is more outlandish, that all of it just happened, or some being designed it all? The Creator God, spoken of in the Old Testament scriptures, has revealed more about Him to affirm His status and to pique anyone's interest. What has become known about Him has been through meetings or encounters. The nature of such meetings has been broadly influenced by His very nature, a mystery. God is a perfect eternal being who made space and time and preferably lives outside them and fills them at the same time. As a Spirit (see John 4: 24), His existence is not well comprehended in our dimension making any meeting with Him a matter under His direct control. God makes Himself known to us. Thus, His meetings are mostly chanced and not planned by us. Any meeting with God, however, is a meeting never to be forgotten. The impression made cannot be truly qualified by expressions made after. Men argue out His existence and fail at it because they make their case and pursue their interests at the fringes of His existence. Here are some of the expressions about God in the Holy Scriptures:

> **Psalm 145:3 (ESV)** – Great is the Lord, and greatly to be praised, and his greatness is unsearchable.
> **1 Chronicles 29:11 (ESV)** – Yours, O Lord, is the greatness and the power and the glory and the victory and the majesty, for all that is in the heavens and in the earth is yours. Yours is the kingdom, O Lord, and you are exalted as head above all.
> **Isaiah 40:26 (NIV)** – Lift up your eyes and look to the heavens: Who created all these? He who brings out the starry host one by one and calls forth each of them by name. Because of his great power and mighty strength, not one of them is missing.
> **Psalm 147:5 (ESV)** – Great is our Lord, and abundant in power; his understanding is beyond measure.
> **Job 37:5** – God thunders marvellously with His voice; He does great things which we cannot comprehend.
> **Psalm 62:11** – God has spoken once, Twice I have heard this: That power belongs to God.

We can only admit to the authors of the above references being the custodians of such revelations on the basis of experiences. A close look at the Holy

Scriptures (Old Testament) therefore does show several meetings between God and men and the resultant impact. There are cases where the meetings were mediated, and such can be found to demonstrate different impressions.

The Case of Abraham

We glean from the scriptures that Abraham, formerly Abram, had direct contact with God who impressed upon him to relocate to a region he was to own for himself and descendants. The actions of this patriarch of the Jews couldn't have been guided by an illusion or an immaculate bouquet of deception and falsehood. He journeyed over a thousand miles with the entire family from Ur to Canaan, all at the behest of God. In the concluding verses of Genesis 11, we learn of Abraham embarking on this journey with his father. Midway through the journey, they settled in Haran where Terah, Abraham's father, died. For anyone making assumptions about the family's journey, they would have thought Terah was the one responding to the command of God after an encounter. In fact, there is a verse which suggests this: "And Terah took his son Abram and his grandson Lot, the son of Haran, and his daughter-in-law Sarai, his son Abram's wife, and they went out with them from Ur of the Chaldeans to go to the land of Canaan; and they came to Haran and dwelt there." (Genesis 11:31). The introductory verses of Genesis chapter 12, however, show that he was not:

> Now the Lord had said to Abram: "Get out of your country, from your family and from your father's house to a land that I will show you. I will make you a great nation; I will bless you and make your name great; And you shall be a blessing. I will bless those who bless you, and I will curse him who curses you; and in you all the families of the earth shall be blessed." (Genesis 12:1-3)

The first line of the above passage clearly reveals Abraham, or Abram, as the one who had received an instruction from God to relocate and not the father. The father did actually get them to settle in Haran which was short of the full distance divinely prescribed. They spent five years there until he died which gave way for the journey to be resumed. It is obvious that anyone with directives from God after a meeting will not settle for just anything or anywhere. There is a consistent clarity to a mission based on a vision received. Evidently, Abraham had met God. The martyred Stephen of the early Church shared this:

> Brethren and fathers, listen: The God of glory appeared to our father Abraham when he was in Mesopotamia, before he dwelt in Haran, and said to him, "Get out of your country and from your relatives, and come to a land that I will show you." Then he came out of the land of the Chaldeans and dwelt in Haran. And from there, when his father was dead, He moved him to this land in which you now dwell. (Acts 7:2-4)

Abraham, on meeting with God, could accept His precepts and trust in His promises. For that, he journeyed for years only to be shown a land and not even have it at the time. His distinctive and characteristic trust or faith in God became his hallmark which could only have been possible because he lived the reality of a relationship with the God he had met. This is why he could go ahead to obediently sacrifice a promised son simply at a command. Imagine this: he heard, without question, God, who never once asked for a human sacrifice, suddenly ask for one, and then he again heard, in the process of offering the sacrifice, the same God ask him to stop the act and turn to a ram already provided in a thicket. The level of promptness, unambiguity and intelligibility exhibited can only suggest a relationship which was real and clear as day. Abraham had certainly met God and had come to know Him. His was a meeting without mediation.

The Case of Jacob

Jacob was the grandson of Abraham and the third in the line of the patriarchs. The circumstances of his birth and even his name aligned him with trickery, supplanting and deceit. He cunningly duped his twin brother, Esau, of his birth right with a bowl of food. As if that was not enough, he finally obtained, with the help of his mother, the covenant blessing of his father Isaac instead of Esau. The covenant blessing bore the promises given by God to Abraham which involved the messianic lineage and divine privilege as the chosen of all men. For a young man coming from a family with its noted relationship with God that was somewhat unseemly. Like many born into Christian homes today, Jacob must have grown up hearing much about God. The thing though is that a party hearing the retelling of a story is not the same as a party experiencing the reality of the story told. Religion of the fathers is more of a tradition than a subjective reality. It was obvious Jacob was yet to meet the God of Abraham. But he would.

When the tension between Jacob and the vexed brother got to a head, he was advised by his mother to relocate to his uncle's place about five hundred miles away. At some point on his solitary journey, he rested at a place for the night. He dreamt he had his head on a stone and beheld the existing reality of a connection (ladder) between heaven and the earth. That was when he met the Lord, God:

> And behold, the Lord stood above it and said: "I am the Lord God of Abraham your father and the God of Isaac; the land on which you lie I will give to you and your descendants. Also your descendants shall be as the dust of the earth; you shall spread abroad to the west and the east, to the north and the south; and in you and in your seed all the families of the earth shall be blessed. Behold, I am with you and will keep you wherever you go and will bring you back to this land; for I will not leave you until I have done what I have spoken to you." (Genesis 28:13-15)

The words seen to be spoken by God to Jacob seemed like a replay of the very same ones to Abraham. Now this is because they featured in the covenant blessing that Jacob now carried. God had come to personally reaffirm the inherit promises in the blessing to the new patriarch, Jacob. His response then unveils his previous convictions and position: "Then Jacob made a vow, saying, 'If God will be with me, and keep me in this way that I am going, and give me bread to eat and clothing to put on, so that I come back to my father's house in peace, **then the Lord shall be my God**.'" (Genesis 28:20-21, emphasis mine). Jacob's response indicates that he had a Lord who was not yet his own. He might have heard or learnt much about the God of his fathers, but He was yet to be his God. His meeting with God did not even generate an instant association or commitment. He wanted to build a personal relationship with God too just like his fathers. God was to be "his God" only when he safely returned to the promised land of Canaan.

The next time Jacob met with God, it was a convincing encounter and one which left a lasting impression. After twenty years with his uncle, Jacob returned to Canaan with a huge family of two wives and possessions. His stay with the uncle had been rife with what always plagued him – fraud and deceit. It was clear Jacob was not really a changed man after his first meeting with God. Some people never are. Besides, he had offered to get truly serious with God when he returned home peacefully. On his return journey, he figured his brother Esau, on hearing about it, might seek revenge. He therefore sent ahead of him some of his possessions as gifts for the brother and divided up the family into parties so that all would not perish should there be any form of reprisal attack from Esau. Typical Jacob. Exceedingly restless the night before the meeting with his brother, Jacob sent everyone away and was left alone. The scriptures say he wrestled with a man that night until dawn which was more of a struggle between himself and God. That was his meeting with God that changed him forever. The incident got his name and form changed. He began the night as Jacob without a limp, but ended it with one, a staff to lean on, and the new name Israel, simply because he had truly met God personally (see Genesis 32:24-31). As a result, the feared meeting with the brother was no longer the supposed meeting between Jacob and Esau, but Israel and Esau which was peaceful and brotherly. Jacob therefore returned to Canaan to make the Lord his God because He had indeed returned him peacefully after their meeting.

The Case of Moses

Jacob and his family ended up in Egypt to join the penultimate son, Joseph, who had become a prime minister of the region. From a small family of just over seventy, the descendants of Jacob became practically a nation of thousands after a period of four hundred years. At this stage, the family of

Jacob, commonly called Israel now, had come under servitude in Egypt. Israel had become Egypt dwellers, conversant with existing lifestyles, customs, and practices. In the cause of their increase and bondage, there was an edict for the violent slaughter of all sons born to Israel. It was under these circumstances that Moses was born. The death threats never deterred the mother from keeping him and later set things up in order to be his nurse on behalf of Pharoah's daughter who adopted him (see Exodus 2:1-10). Moses therefore began as a child of Israel and matured into a prince of Egypt. A meeting with his people one day stirred within him a desire to seek their interest and cause. He felt like a deliverer before he was called one. This interest caused his unfortunate murder of an Egyptian he found beating a Hebrew one day. The result was a sudden flight from the region to escape the wrath of Pharaoh. Moses obviously attempted a feat which he was not yet called or assigned to, and the consequence was failure.

    The flight from Egypt brought Moses to the family of Jethro and a life different from the one he had grown accustomed to. Now, as a shepherd, he learnt to patiently and devotedly cater for a flock that was never his own (see Exodus 3:1). To lead a people, he had to learn to lead a flock of sheep. From a prince to a shepherd, Moses needed to be reequipped to lead Israel which had become lost in the midst of its slavery and assimilation in Egypt; a flock needing a shepherd. It was only at that point could he meet with the one who calls to divine assignment or pursuit. When God scheduled a meeting with Moses, it was done with such flamboyance, and you may wonder why. Moses had lived for forty years in Egypt, a world power then, experiencing opulence, sophistication and wonder. Then he had to live another forty years in Midian as a shepherd roaming the wilderness with nothing of interest or significance. A person like that, seeing both extremes, would need the profound to be found and that is what the burning bush achieved: "So when the Lord saw that he turned aside to look, God called to him from the midst of the bush and said, 'Moses, Moses!' And he said, 'Here I am.'" (Exodus 3:4). It is obvious that God knows how to make an impression in his meetings. Jacob had to wrestle with Him like a man would and Moses had to see a display of His glory and wonder. Two different meetings with different modes but both befitting the existing circumstances and characters involved.

Like all other cited meetings, God's meeting with Moses was purposeful and, in his case, involved an assignment for him to return to Egypt to liberate the people of Israel. He was to be a deliverer not by interest but by divine calling and instruction. He left home that morning as a shepherd of a flock, powerless and with a staff that could only guide and guard his sheep, but returned as a mandated shepherd of a people with a staff that literally bore the power he had suddenly been given. That is what a meeting with God does, it transforms.

The Case of Israel

We can boldly surmise that Abraham, Jacob and Moses had direct contact with God. Their meetings started the course and advancement of a nation and collective destinies. The meeting of Israel as a people with God was cast in complex circumstances. After centuries of life in Egypt, little is said of their level of knowledge or even relationship with the God of their fathers. When God instructed Moses to return to Egypt for them, he asked, "If I go to the people of Israel and tell them, 'The God of your ancestors has sent me to you,' they will ask me, 'What is his name?' Then what should I tell them?" (Exodus 3:13 NLT). The legitimacy of Moses' protest was never in question but there was a problem. God never had a prevailing relationship with the people directly and so could only ask him to tell them that "I am" had sent him and in fact, "Yahweh, the God of your ancestors—the God of Abraham, the God of Isaac, and the God of Jacob—has sent me to you." (Exodus 3:15 NLT). God was not yet their God since they were yet to meet. He was to be "I am" until their meeting determined how they wished to qualify Him.

To add to this complexity, God was to be introduced to Israel by a runaway prince who had recently met Him. Moses never had much to say but had a lot of wonders to do before the people and against Egypt. His "acts of God" somehow laid the basis of the people's new found knowledge of God. This made a lasting imprint which set up another complexity. After many wonders by God in Egypt at the hands of Moses, Israel finally made it out of the region to begin a new life with God who had recently been introduced to them with mighty demonstrations of power and unparalleled magnificence. They still needed to meet with God and a prior appointment had been made for them at Mount Sinai: "Then the Lord said to Moses, 'Go to the people and consecrate them today and tomorrow, and let them wash their clothes. And let them be ready for the third day. For on the third day the Lord will come down upon Mount Sinai in the sight of all the people.'" (Exodus 19:10-11). God did come on the third day: "Then it came to pass on the third day, in the morning, that there were thunderings and lightnings, and a thick cloud on the mountain; and the sound of the trumpet was very loud, so that all the people who were in the camp trembled. And Moses brought the people out of the camp to meet with God, and they stood at the foot of the mountain." (Exodus 19:16-17). Now there was the meeting. God showed up for his meeting with the people of Israel directly for the first time. And the meeting was spectacular for the very same reason that Moses' own was. Israel had seen the splendour and demonstrated powers of Egypt's deities for years and so needed something more stunning to attract their attention. It goes without saying that God did get their attention and possibly the worse kind: "Now all the people witnessed the thunderings, the lightning flashes, the sound of the trumpet, and the mountain smoking; and when the people saw it, they trembled and stood afar off. Then they said to Moses, 'You speak with us, and we will hear; but let not God speak with us, lest we die.'" (Exodus 19:18-19). So, the people did have a meeting but shrunk from contact. They actually withdrew from the presence of God while Moses went before Him on their behalf. This clearly began the system of mediation between God and the people. Israel met God but chose not to carry on a relationship with Him directly. The consequence was grave, and this would affect the people's relationship with God for many, many generations (see Isaiah 29:13; Matthew 15:8).

The Case of a God

There is an interesting story shared in scriptures concerning a meeting between God and another god. As expected, the meeting was not without its impact and the setting without an element of surprise. The story is recounted in chapter 5 of the book of 1 Samuel. In said story, which starts out from the previous chapter, Israel rallies into battle against their archenemies at the time. They lost the battle to the Philistines with the loss of four thousand men. Despondent and grief-stricken, the people deliberated on their predicament and concluded that they needed God in their midst, as if He wasn't there already. This was part of the fallout of the failure of their fathers to relate to God without any mediation or intervention. To relate to God, they had to relate to an ark. The elders of Israel therefore asked for the Ark of the Covenant to be brought in from Shiloh. At the time, the presence of the Ark practically signified the presence of God. Just like every signification or symbol, the Ark wasn't God, neither God the Ark. The Ark stood in for God and invoked His presence when needed. So, to have the Ark of God, or Covenant, in battle was pragmatically to have God in battle. The Ark was brought in and that was a first.

> And when the ark of the covenant of the Lord came into the camp, all Israel shouted so loudly that the earth shook. Now when the Philistines heard the noise of the shout, they said, "What does the sound of this great shout in the camp of the Hebrews mean?" Then they understood that the ark of the Lord had come into the camp. So the Philistines were afraid, for they said, "God has come into the camp!" And they said, "Woe to us! For such a thing has never happened before." (1 Samuel 4:5-7)

Israel lost the next battle with the Philistines even with God supposedly amongst them. The Ark was captured, the sons of the priests keeping the Ark were killed, and their father, the high priest, collapsed and died on hearing the news. That was a strange turn of events ending with "God being captured" but it begins our story of interest. The Philistines placed the Ark in the temple of their chief god, Dagon. It is obvious the people felt the Ark, being an item of religious significance, was best stowed away in said temple. Unknown to the people, they had set up a meeting between their god and the God of Israel with disastrous consequences. Dagon, the central idol of the Philistines, was shaped from stone and depicted a deity who was half-fish and half-man. Surviving images resemble a mermaid with a

Sumerian-style beard. The signification of Dagon pointed to created things, making him essentially a created entity. His meeting with the Creator could only end one way. No one stands in the presence of the God of Abraham, Isaac, Jacob or Israel without offering worship or bowing. Nothing. (see Nehemiah 9:6; Psalm 5:7; Zephaniah 2:11).

Dagon certainly never called nor asked for the meeting with God but that didn't change the outcome. He bowed and was found so. Trouble was, his people didn't realise what was going on and so, finding him prostrate before the Ark of God, they restored him to his position. What happened next would change his status and even his people's worship of him:

> Then the Philistines took the ark of God and brought it from Ebenezer to Ashdod. When the Philistines took the ark of God, they brought it into the house of Dagon and set it by Dagon. And when the people of Ashdod arose early in the morning, there was Dagon, fallen on its face to the earth before the ark of the Lord. So they took Dagon and set it in its place again. And when they arose early the next morning, there was Dagon, fallen on its face to the ground before the ark of the Lord. The head of Dagon and both the palms of its hands were broken off on the threshold; only Dagon's torso was left of it. Therefore neither the priests of Dagon nor any who come into Dagon's house tread on the threshold of Dagon in Ashdod to this day. (1 Samuel 5:1-5)

There is a striking similitude in this story and that of Jacob's. He struggled with God and ended up with a dislocated hip and Dagon apparently did likewise and ended up dismembered. Who gets to make a light matter of a meeting with God? What can remain unaffected by such a meeting? God always makes an impression in His meetings.

Meeting God is obviously a possibility and can be pursued. However, unlike planned meetings, a meeting with God cannot be predetermined. As earlier indicated, it is sudden and preferred by God to be direct. The commonly known meetings are the mediated ones where we get to meet God through the experience of another. That is remarkable all right but bears no semblance to a direct encounter. We will find out later in these pages that God has a definite interest in direct meetings and has even made the effort to make that a prevailing possibility.

Reflection

1. *Assess now*: What knowledge do you have of God? Is your knowledge mostly from human sources and means? Has that created an image and person of God in your mind and how is that image? Have you met anyone who has met God or claimed same or have you yourself? Have you given the experience any special thought or place before now? Do you agree God will make an impression in any meeting with Him?

2. *Consider now*: Knowledge of God is not necessarily a validation or evidence of an experience of Him. Most of the human sources of shared stories of divine experiences or encounters are mediated and of related narratives across generations. Anyone sharing or writing about a meeting with God as heard from another can never deliver the same effect as when shared by the direct witness. Would you consider a mediated encounter with God or a personal one? Given the opportunity, would you want to meet God through a "Moses" or meet Him yourself? It is evident that God can be met and a meeting with Him ultimately leaves an impression. Would you deem it possible for someone to meet with God directly and live oblivious to His reality and go against His ways and will? Wouldn't it be fair or even right to find out the reason and motivation for such a case should you know one? Remember there is a difference between Moses' meeting with God and Israel's meeting with Him. Is your interest piqued now to meet God if you haven't already?

Chapter 4

Meeting Jesus, The Son of God

The Old Testament offers us the clearest instances of God's meetings with mankind as cited in the previous chapter. In fact, the beginning was even different. We see from the instance of the garden of Eden that man could practically hear the footsteps of God (see Genesis 3:8). God walked and man heard, which reveals the extent and depth of man's relationship with Him at the time. Man's loss of the garden caused by his disobedience or sin before God led all humanity from His presence and His reality. So, man moved on from essentially chatting to God to praying to Him by mostly looking up. How far away God appeared to be, not within reach, but often hosted in imaginations. We learn that as man moved away from God, He reached out to him along the way. God was excited and pleased with Noah and so picked him and his family to start a new era after an apocalyptic flood. Abraham also got picked to start a new nation that was to be an example of God's reign centred on the relationship with a people. All this was not without challenges. Many have always regarded God as the bearded, judgemental, exalted being, removed from mankind's daily realities, frailties and difficulties. I have heard it said many times that, "God is up there with no idea as to what we really go through down here". That may have some validity but there are noted cases of God showing up tangibly before some people. He showed up at the tent of Abraham directly promising the birth of Isaac before having his angels go on to destroy Sodom and Gomorrah (Genesis 18:1-33). There is another instance where, when three Hebrew young men got thrown into a fiery furnace because they refused to bow to an idol of Nebuchadnezzar, God was seen in the midst of them by the king as the "Son of God" (Daniel 3:25 KJV).

The not so simple question which then gets asked is, "Has anyone seen God physically before?". The two examples cited above should fairly indicate that some have but could that have been God since, firstly, He is a Spirit and secondly, He mentioned to Moses that, "You cannot see My face; for no man shall see Me, and live." (Exodus 33:20). How does mankind get to see God who is always on His throne? Is there a form of Him that we get to see? Many biblical scholars and expositors have advanced the point drawn from Apostle Paul's teaching of God having an observable image of His invisible Self. According to Paul, Jesus is, "the image of the invisible God, the firstborn over all creation." (Colossians 1:15). In effect, when Jesus shows up for a meeting, that is God physically showing up for that meeting. Thus, Nebuchadnezzar was not wrong when he said he had seen the Son of God (Jesus, unbeknownst to him at the time) in the midst of the flames with the Hebrew young men. Jesus made sense of it all when He said, "I and My Father are one." (John 10:30). Again, we have the writer of the letter to the Hebrews in the New Testament throw more light on this by saying:

> God, who at various times and in various ways spoke in time past to the fathers by the prophets, has in these last days spoken to us by His Son, whom He has appointed heir of all things, through whom also He made the worlds; who being the brightness of His glory and the express image of His person, and upholding all things by the word of His power, when He had by Himself purged our sins, sat down at the right hand of the Majesty on high, having become so much better than the angels, as He has by inheritance obtained a more excellent name than they. (Hebrews 1:1-4)

So Who Is Jesus?

To begin with, there is a pending faith and reality that Jesus cannot be cited or referenced in the past, given the fact and belief he is alive, once dead but resurrected and now living. So introducing him now will not be cast in the past or framed in antiquity. Jesus, simply put, is the Son of God whose birth was shrouded in mystery which involved angelic visitations and prophesies. The key point is, God needed to manifest Himself amongst humanity unlike before when He had occasional meetings with particular individuals. He might have showed up mysteriously in past instances, but He wanted to dwell for a time amongst men to fix a broken relationship. As previously mentioned, if He was once said to be up there, He wanted to be down here to have our unique experiences and overcome what no one else could. To come in amongst men, God needed to be a man, which required Him being born as a man. So by prophesy, "'Behold, the virgin shall be with child, and bear a Son, and they shall call His name Immanuel,' which is translated, 'God with us.'" (Matthew 1:23). Jesus was therefore born of a virgin called Mary under the unction of God's Holy Spirit without human intervention (see Luke 1:35). Hence Jesus was adopted by a human father, Joseph, since he never had one. God is the Father and one with Him.

His Story in History

The story of Jesus has primarily had one source which is the New Testament. As such, any contention with this Testament alludes to a contestation of the story. However, there is historical evidence to the story and existence of the person of Jesus. He is a Hebrew or Jew, born in the land of Palestine during the reign of Caesar Augustus (63 BC–14 AD), which are all not elements of fiction. In fact, within a few decades of his lifetime, Jesus was mentioned by Jewish and Roman historians in passages that corroborate portions of the New Testament that describe his life and death. The first-century Jewish historian, Flavius Josephus, who is regarded by most as possibly the best source of information about first-century Palestine, twice mentions Jesus in *Jewish Antiquities*, his massive twenty-volume history of the Jewish people that was written around 93 AD. Josephus was a well-connected aristocrat and military leader in Palestine who served as a commander in Galilee during the first Jewish Revolt against Rome between 66 and 70 AD. In one passage of *Jewish Antiquities* that relates an unlawful execution, Josephus identifies the victim, James, as the "brother of Jesus-who-is-called-Messiah". Josephus further wrote a lengthier passage about Jesus, known as the *Testimonium*

Flavianum, which describes a man "who did surprising deeds" and was condemned to be crucified by Pilate.

Another account of Jesus appears in the *Annals of Imperial Rome*, a first-century history of the Roman Empire written around 116 AD by the Roman senator and historian, Tacitus. In recounting the burning of Rome in 64 AD, Tacitus mentions that Emperor Nero falsely blamed "the persons commonly called Christians, who were hated for their enormities. Christus, the founder of the name, was put to death by Pontius Pilate, procurator of Judea in the reign of Tiberius". Shortly before Tacitus penned his account of Jesus, Roman governor Pliny the Younger wrote to Emperor Trajan that early Christians would "sing hymns to Christ as to a god". Now these were historians and dignified state officials who clearly wrote about verifiable facts and were not swayed by personal biases. We learn from them that Jesus is not just a person of New Testament accounts, with of course some Christian biases, but of authentic history and records.

Meeting Jesus

Meetings with Jesus have a character not different from God's. They easily and quickly make an impression, and they are gripping and lasting. The first recorded incident of a meeting with Jesus occurred when he was still in the womb of the mother:

> Now Mary arose in those days and went into the hill country with haste, to a city of Judah, and entered the house of Zacharias and greeted Elizabeth. And it happened, when Elizabeth heard the greeting of Mary, that the babe leaped in her womb; and Elizabeth was filled with the Holy Spirit. Then she spoke out with a loud voice and said, "Blessed are you among women, and blessed is the fruit of your womb!" (Luke 1:39-42)

The above passage points to a meeting between Elizabeth, the mother of John the Baptist, and Mary, the mother of Jesus. Looked at closely enough, however, it was, in fact, a meeting between Jesus and John. The impact was immediate and noticeable. We see Elizabeth suddenly filled with the Holy Spirit, the very Spirit of Jesus, and by an obvious leading of the Spirit, she declares the same words spoken to Mary by the angel during the announcement of the conception of Jesus. The transformative character of a meeting with Jesus is seen in this instance. The same character will be evident in the numerous meetings Jesus had with various groups and people. In some cases, the transformative effect wasn't manifest, but there was an impressive effect, nonetheless.

The Case of the Teachers

At the age of twelve, Jesus was reported to have met with the teachers of the law. The meeting was summed up as amazing: "Now so it was that after three days they found Him in the temple, sitting in the midst of the teachers, both listening to them and asking them questions. And all who heard Him were astonished at His understanding and answers." (Luke 2:46-47). One can only imagine the nature of the discourse Jesus was having with the scholars at the time on the intricate system of the law. I would have loved to spectate. This incidence is a reported first but was definitely not the last. Throughout his ministry, Jesus had frequent run-ins with the teachers of the law who considered him obnoxious and annoying, simply because he couldn't be challenged by them on any question of the law. This was their preferred response instead of admitting to his depth of understanding and wisdom. They just refused at all costs to be impressed. However, some did: "There was a man of the Pharisees named Nicodemus, a ruler of the Jews. This man came to Jesus by night and said to Him, 'Rabbi, we know that You are a teacher come from God; for no one can do these signs that You do unless God is with him.'" (John 3:1-2). Nicodemus practically acceded to Jesus' personality and calling, and offered a hint of the collective view of others, possibly his colleagues.

We know the persistent rejection and intolerable view of Jesus will eventually drive the teachers of the law together with some highly placed members of the Jewish priesthood to seek his crucifixion. That proved to be an unfamiliar resort but a favoured one nonetheless given the circumstances. The teachers just wanted Jesus out of the way so badly. It was a classic case of hating a prey for missing it in a hunt.

The Case of the Disciples

Jesus chose his disciples (see John 15:16) which was done through meetings. Of the twelve disciples that officially became Jesus' stewards and closest followers, most had remarkable encounters with him prior to discipleship. Nathaniel (Bartholomew) had such a meeting after he got Jesus introduced to him by Philip. Now Philip, on the other hand, just had to be asked by Jesus to follow him. One tends to ask what could make an individual with responsibilities and possible commitments follow another just by asking. When Nathaniel was told about Jesus he doubted, to which Philip simply said, "Come and see." (John 1:46). I guess that is the likeliest response when there is nothing to be said but only experienced. Jesus saw Nathanael coming towards Him, and said of him, "'Behold, an Israelite indeed, in whom is no deceit!' Nathanael said to Him, 'How do You know me?' Jesus answered and said to him, 'Before Philip called you when you were under the fig tree, I saw you.'" (John 1:47-48). The response to follow was that of someone who had just been impressed, "Nathanael answered and said to Him, 'Rabbi, You are the Son of God! You are the King of Israel!'" (John 49). That is the level and measure of impact a meeting with Jesus is able to make. It overwhelms, disrupts existing orders, and invokes devotion.

The positively disruptive nature of a meeting with Jesus is seen in other encounters with some of the disciples: "As Jesus passed on from there, He saw a man named Matthew sitting at the tax office. And He said to him, 'Follow Me.' So he arose and followed Him." (Matthew 9:9). How easy was that? Think of an official of the state engaged in a role that possibly offered a good income and job security who is suddenly asked to relinquish all that and does so within a heartbeat. What could have caused such an act if not a profound stimulus or the disruptive effect of an encounter – a Jesus meeting. It turns plans on their head, and changes life courses only to set new paths. Peter's meeting with Jesus had the same effect. He met Jesus in the cause of the day as a fisherman and ended it as a "fisher of men" (see Luke 5:1-11). His fruitless efforts at sea previously with his team were miraculously changed at the words and instructions of Jesus. A night of no fish was changed into a day of abundant fish just by meeting Jesus. At this, he, together with James and John, the sons of Zebedee, "forsook all and followed Him." (see Luke 5:11). Imagine this – they left everything.

The Case of the Samaritan Woman

John tells a story in the fourth chapter of his gospel of a meeting between Jesus and a woman from Samaria (see John 4:4-26). Jesus had stopped at a city in Samaria with His disciples to get some refreshments when the meeting happened. Now, there was a severe rift between Jews and the Samaritans at the time on matters of religious worship and beliefs. In fact, the hatred amongst these parties festered to the point of causing mutual avoidance. No contact was entertained. This served as the premise of Jesus' parable of the "Good Samaritan" and its definition of a neighbour (see Luke 10:25-37). So, in the first place, it was unusual for Jesus and His team to enter a Samaritan city and secondly, for Him to be found by his disciples engaged with one of the local women by a well. This points to another character of Jesus' meetings, which is non-discriminatory. He is ready to meet with anybody.

The conversation held by Jesus with the Samaritan, who was never named, was relatively topical. It transitioned from the social to the religious. These were the trending issues and notions which bothered Jews and Samaritans alike. They were the matters of contact and worship. Jesus' response to both was insightful and truly puzzling to the woman. He simply directed her attention to the lack of understanding held by all on the subject. What was known at the time was completely deficient of the whole truth even though the Jews had some of it. He essentially disrupted the held knowledge and notions with His higher knowledge. This caused Him to speak of some truth known only to the woman just to affirm His superior knowledge and insight. She had had five husbands and was cohabiting with a man at the time. That did say enough about her social and religious standing unlike the individual she was contesting. Her instant inference was, "Sir, I perceive that You are a prophet." (John 4:19). Clearly impressed and converted, "the woman then left her waterpot, went her way into the city, and said to the men, 'Come, see a Man who told me all things that I ever did. Could this be the Christ?' Then they went out of the city and came to Him." (John

28-30). So, the Samaritan woman met Jesus, was impacted by the meeting and, as is always the case, left all she had so she could explore her new finding. Hers was to get the people of the city to share in her experience by meeting with the one she had found. Here we probably have our first official New Testament evangelist revealed.

The Case of Paul

Paul considered himself as the late entrant to the apostolic scene. He did meet Jesus but not in the way the other apostles or disciples did. Paul had an interesting meeting with Jesus, and it was all after playing an anti-Christian role for some time. He was known to be zealous for the law, a Pharisee, and a persecutor of the early Church (see Philippians 3:6). As a matter of fact, he is introduced in the Scriptures as a witness to the murder of Stephen, the first recorded martyr of the early Church (see Acts 7:58). He was known then as Saul. His exploits gained traction which caused the interest to extend them beyond the boundaries of Jerusalem. Thus, it was on his way to Damascus to round up more members of the growing Church when he met Jesus. There is good reason to think or even assume that Paul had heard about the story of Jesus and the obvious stand of the religious authorities. Like most people today, he had met Jesus but indirectly. It is said that, "As he journeyed, he came near Damascus, and suddenly a light shone around him from heaven. Then he fell to the ground, and heard a voice saying to him, 'Saul, Saul, why are you persecuting Me?' And he said, 'Who are You, Lord?' Then the Lord said, 'I am Jesus, whom you are persecuting. It is hard for you to kick against the goads.'" (Acts 9:3-5).

The effect of Jesus' meeting with Paul was full of its known characteristics. It was impactful, disruptive, and transformative. He could never deny what he had experienced and even had witnesses (see Acts 9:7). The meeting left him blind because truly that was his spiritual state. What he thought he knew and strongly upheld was nothing but pieces of misguided facts and doctored lore. He might have been religiously agile, but he was spiritually lethargic. What he ended up doing massively attested to the conversion experience he had in his meeting with Jesus. Like Abram who became Abraham, Saul became Paul and transitioned from a persecutor of Christ's followers to a promoter of His ways. This was a man who laid bare his sufferings for the pursuit of the cause of Christ and the Kingdom of God:

> Are they Hebrews? So am I. Are they Israelites? So am I. Are they offspring of Abraham? So am I. Are they servants of Christ? I am a better one—I am talking like a madman—with far greater labors, far more imprisonments, with countless beatings, and often near death. Five times I received at the hands of the Jews the forty lashes less one. Three times I was beaten with rods. Once I was stoned. Three times I was shipwrecked; a night and a day I was adrift at sea; on frequent journeys, in danger from rivers, danger from robbers, danger from my own people, danger from Gentiles, danger in the city, danger in the wilderness, danger at sea, danger from false brothers; in toil and hardship, through many a sleepless night, in hunger and thirst, often without food in cold and exposure. (2 Corinthians 11:22-27)

Only one thing can be said about a person who accepts to pursue a mission on the back of such named threats, sufferings, and dangers – an unquestionable conviction. Paul had definitely met Jesus, been convicted, and converted, and was ready to be a witness at all costs. What else could have been the grounds for his actions and desire to "know him and the power of his resurrection, and may share his sufferings, becoming like him in his death" (Philippians 3:10)? It could only have been a meeting with Jesus Christ, the Son of God.

Reflection

1. *Assess now*: Have you been part of the crowd that perceives God as absent from our affairs and removed from our reality? Do you believe Jesus to be the Son of God? How have you regarded the relationship between Jesus and God? Are you convinced that Jesus' coming into our world was God showing up in the midst of men? Do you believe you have met Jesus and thus met God? What would you say of the experience?

2. *Consider now*: The enduring Scriptures bear witness to the life and work of Jesus. There are historical records to suggest the same. Jesus came into our world, introduced it to the Kingdom of God and was crucified for the sins of all mankind so all can be reconciled with God. His followers carried on His work as the Church which has outlived every form of persecution, resistance and affliction. This can only point to the truth and authenticity of what had been experienced and embraced. Jesus can be nothing but real to His witnesses. All who have met Him cannot deny His reality and power. There is enough to suggest that no one meets Jesus and ever remains the same. Such tends to either persecute Him or promote Him, but the one that directly meets with Him is certainly bound to embrace Him and to be a gallant witness. So, a Christian is a believer of Christ, who has met Him and has had a personal experience of His reality and ready to share this truth. The same would be a transformed individual with definite changes and unquestionable conviction. This is the new person in Christ.

Chapter 5

Meeting The Holy Spirit, The Spirit of God

There is a clear pattern when one studies the Holy Scriptures about God's interactions with mankind. The pattern lends itself to three sets of periods or epochs. There is the period mostly related in the Old Testament, where we had God, the Father, interact or engage with mankind. This is followed by the period of the New Testament, where God is revealed amongst humanity as His Son, Jesus. Then there is the last and present epoch which has God interact with His people by His Spirit. The prophet Joel was alluding to this when he prophesied that, "And it shall come to pass afterward That I will pour out My Spirit on all flesh; Your sons and your daughters shall prophesy, Your old men shall dream dreams, Your young men shall see visions. And also on My menservants and on My maidservants I will pour out My Spirit in those days." (Joel 2:28-29). The various periods seem to point to the intention of God to remain involved with His creations and not to be an "absentee Creator" as some aim to suggest. It appears God has been reaching out to men since they turned away from Him in the beginning (see Romans 1:20). He has been there as the Father, came down as the Son and then filled all men who allowed Him as the Holy Spirit. It is as if He is, as Jesus mentioned, not leaving His own ever comfortless or fatherless, "I will not leave you comfortless: I will come to you." (John 14:18 KJV).

Who Is He?

The Holy Spirit is simply the Spirit of God. He is explicitly God. He is never a thing or an entity that gets to be related to God. He is completely God as a Spirit. He is easily known in many quarters as the third person of the Trinity, a complex concept of God which has lent itself to many debates and contentions over the years. We find the Trinity especially revealed at the baptism of Jesus when God spoke, and the Holy Spirit descended on Jesus as a dove (see Luke 3:2-22). Here you get the three all present. The easiest way to explain the Trinity is to use the nature of man. Made in the image of God, man also has the same three forms. Every man is practically a spirit with a soul that lives in a body – a tripartite being. As long as man is alive and animatedly existent, none of his three parts are independently extant although individually unique and functional. The point here is, the body is not the soul, nor the soul the spirit. They all make you function as you, but in unique ways. At the funeral of any dead man, we have present before all a body, yet we admit the person is departed. Why? Because the spirit and soul which animates the body is completely separated from it.

God has this very nature of man. He is three in one. We could illustrate that God is like the soul of man, Jesus is the body that gets seen and the Holy Spirit is like our spirit that brings all together. Truth is, you are more of your spirit than any other part since the spirit is the core. Every human essence is enlivened by the spirit. In the same way, God is practically His Spirit and He is holy. Just as your spirit is not easily available to be toyed with so the Holy Spirit cannot be trifled with. Jesus enlightened us about the gravity of the matter when He said that, "Anyone who speaks a word against the Son of Man, it will be forgiven him; but whoever speaks against the Holy Spirit, it will not be forgiven him, either in this age or in the age to come." (Matthew 12:32). This obviously throws in an exception to the rule of God's forgiveness. Once thought to be boundless, here we gather that there is no forgiveness for any blasphemy against God's Spirit. He must be exceptionally special.

The Holy Spirit was there during creation "hovering over the face of the waters" (Genesis 1:1). As a Spirit, He is, but then can only be represented. He is never what depicts Him. So He is never a dove (see Matthew 3:16), a wind (see Acts 2:2), a breadth (see John 20:22), fire (see Acts 2:3-4), wine (see Ephesians 5:18), or water (see Isaiah 44:3; John 4:14). These may be His representations or means of manifestation but not Him. Failure to acknowledge this often leads to the error of considering the Holy Spirit as a thing, unrelatable and even fictive. But He is real, extant and has many known attributes and gifts. He is described as a Helper or Comforter, who is to abide with the people of God forever (see John 14:16), a Teacher or Expositor (see John 16:13), one who grieves (see Ephesians 4:30) and a giver of gifts (see 1 Corinthians 12:8-11). It is obvious He cannot be a thing based on the preceding.

His Era and Role

The Holy Spirit is God here and now. As previously noted from a prophesy of Joel, God had promised not to occasionally contact men or live amongst them as Jesus did anymore, but to remain in contact by living in them. This He is to do by His Spirit. So Jesus confessed that, "I tell you the truth. It is to your advantage that I go away; for if I do not go away, the Helper **(Holy Spirit)** will not come to you; but if I depart, I will send Him to you." (John 16:7). The Holy Spirit therefore took over from Jesus and His goals or intentions were indicated by Jesus:

> And when He has come, He will convict the world of sin, and of righteousness, and of judgment: of sin, because they do not believe in Me; of righteousness, because I go to My Father and you see Me no more; of judgment, because the ruler of this world is judged … However, when He, the Spirit of truth, has come, He will guide you into all truth; for He will not speak on His own authority, but whatever He hears He will speak; and He will tell you things to come. He will glorify Me, for He will take of what is Mine and declare it to you. All things that the Father has are Mine. Therefore I said that He will take of Mine and declare it to you. (John 16:8-11; 13-15)

Primarily, the Holy Spirit is here now to carry on the work of Christ of seeking and saving the lost (see Luke 19:10). He is the Jesus we now get to meet, the God we encounter. He is the one that makes a believer, by convicting same, and maintains till the day of glory. In fact, it is in Him all born-again believers are "sealed for the day of redemption" (Ephesians 4:30). The following typifies the role of the Holy Spirit:

He Convicts the World of Sin – "And when He has come, He will convict the world of sin, and of righteousness, and of judgment: of sin, because they do not believe in Me." (John 16:8-9). Every man has the tendency to go on the defensive when issues of their sins are raised. It isn't simple or even likely for anyone to easily admit to a wrongdoing. We seem to find safety in being dismissive. The Holy Spirit is always exposed to our sins and does the work of convicting us of them. In effect, we convert (are born-again) because He convicts. Thus, no one comes to accept the need for salvation without the Holy Spirit. He essentially brings us to the saving grace of our Lord Jesus Christ. He makes Jesus and His works a reality.

He Is a Helper, Teacher and Counsellor – "But the Helper, the Holy Spirit, whom the Father will send in My name, He will teach you all things, and bring to your remembrance all things that I said to you." (John 14:26). The Greek word *parakletos* in this passage is translated as "Helper" in the ESV, "Advocate" in the NIV, and "Counsellor" in the KJV. The meaning of this word renders "legal counsel". The Holy Spirit as an advocate to the Church ensures it receives wise counsel and insight on matters pertaining to God's will and affairs. His revelatory function brings to the Church what cannot be ascertained through logic or human experience. He is more like a tutor who explains Christ's lectures. As the Spirit behind the Bible, He is apt in bringing it to life and relating its deeper meanings. I have heard amazing and miraculous stories about His teaching prowess – for instance, bringing understanding of the Scriptures to those who wouldn't be considered capable or endowed for such a feat; helping the illiterate to read and comprehend the local language versions of the Bible and even that of English.

He Is the Source of Revelation, Wisdom, and Power – "But God has revealed them to us through His Spirit. For the Spirit searches all things, yes, the deep things of God. For what man knows the things of a man except the spirit of the man which is in him? Even so no one knows the things of God except the Spirit of God." (1 Corinthians 2:10-11). There is an African adage which says that when the catfish comes out of the river to announce the death of a crocodile, there is no need to contest it. The Holy

Spirit is of God and certainly knows all that relates to Him. The truths and revelations which He shares can be just that, the truth. He is the source of wisdom and power which are typically some of the deep things of God. He makes these available and usable.

He Is a Guide to All Truth, Particularly Knowledge of What Is to Come – "However, when He, the Spirit of truth, has come, He will guide you into all truth; for He will not speak on His own authority, but whatever He hears He will speak; and He will tell you things to come." (John 16:13). The Holy Spirit is inherently truthful. He cannot be wrong. His presence in the life of a born-again believer and the Church is to always point to the truth and align all things to it. When certain wrongs are sighted in the body of Christ, it is either the Holy Spirit being ignored or avoided. You must find truth where you find Him. Again, He relates what is to come which keeps His people well informed and never in the dark.

He Dwells in Believers (the Church) and Fills Them – "Do you not know that you are the temple of God and that the Spirit of God dwells in you?" (1 Corinthians 3:16). God once made a promise through the Prophet Joel that He would pour His Spirit on all flesh in the last days (see Joel 2:28) and this He certainly did on the day of Pentecost and thereafter (see Acts 2:1-4). By this, we don't have God showing up occasionally to his people or sending messages through some chosen prophets, or keeping an appearance as an Ark that was stowed away behind curtains or as Jesus walking amongst His own without them knowing He was God, but maintaining real-time presence in the individual lives of His people by residing in them. So, by His Spirit, He comes home. Jesus put it this way, "If anyone loves Me, he will keep My word; and My Father will love him, and We will come to him and make Our home with him." (John 14:23).

He Gives Spiritual Gifts to Born-Again Believers – "There are diversities of gifts, but the same Spirit. But the manifestation of the Spirit is given to each one for the profit of all." (1 Corinthians 12: 4,7). Apostle Paul cites nine gifts in the referred text which the Holy Spirit is known to offer as gifts to believers. These gifts are given according to the will and inclinations of the Holy Spirit and for the benefit of all in the body of Christ or Church. Which means it is never for personal aggrandizement or pleasure. A person can have one or several as the Spirit wills. It is also noteworthy to highlight the point that He still offers these gifts because He still fills and lives with the Church and in believers. The other point of interest is that Jesus practically exhibited most of these gifts during His days of ministry before His ascension with the obvious cause being the Holy Spirit who descended upon Him after His baptism. It is therefore reasonable to see the same Holy Spirit come in to help the Church carry on with Christ's ministry and mission.

He Sanctifies and Empowers Believers to Bear Good Fruits – "But the fruit of the Spirit is love, joy, peace, longsuffering, kindness, goodness, faithfulness, gentleness, self-control. Against such there is no law. If we live in the Spirit, let us also walk in the Spirit." (Galatians 5:22-23, 25). A believer at the point of spiritual conversion is justified by the redeeming work of Christ which in fact begins a process of reformation and transformation. This process, which lasts a lifetime, helps to sanctify the believer and makes the same capable of bearing good fruits and to live as Christ lived. The likelihood of achieving good fruits consistently without the help of God, in this case His Spirit, has been determined by many as far-fetched or next to impracticable. Christ lived full of the Holy Spirit and by that exercised divine grace and power, and the believer can too by the same Spirit.

Meeting the Holy Spirit

The Holy Spirit is the third Person of the Trinity and a meeting with Him is simply a meeting with God. Before the day of Pentecost, the Holy Spirit could only be met on rare occasions. Such meetings were mostly required when God needed to directly empower or enable a person for His work or cause. Like any other meeting with God, His is also transformative and overwhelming. Known cases referenced in the Bible about His meetings always relate to His "coming upon" an individual. The usual result is the individual becoming "another person". We have the instance of Samson who was an ordinary man until the Holy Spirit came upon him: "When he came to Lehi, the Philistines came shouting against him. Then the **Spirit of the Lord came mightily upon him**; and the ropes that were on his arms became like flax that is burned with fire, and his bonds broke loose from his hands. He found a fresh jawbone of a donkey, reached out his hand and took it, and killed a thousand men with it." (Judges 15:14-15, emphasis mine). There is the other case involving King Saul. He had met the Prophet Samuel when searching for missing donkeys and got anointed as the first king of Israel. The prophet then foretold him what was to happen: "Then the **Spirit of the Lord will come upon you**, and you will prophesy with them and **be turned into another man**. And let it be, when these signs come to you, that you do as the occasion demands; for God is with you." (1 Samuel 10:6-7, emphasis mine). The noted effect of a meeting with the Holy Spirit is seen here to be consistent.

As indicated earlier, Jesus also had the Holy Spirit "come upon" Him after getting baptised in the Jordon River. He is known to have been led into the wilderness by the Holy Spirit thereafter to be tempted by the devil. It is fair to assume that the timing was intentional. Jesus never embarked on this exercise in all His thirty years of life on Earth until He was empowered by the Holy Spirit which clearly couldn't be coincidental. He only met the devil first-hand when He had the power to. In fact, it can be argued that His meeting with the devil was a meeting between the devil and the Holy Spirit, the powerhouse of God. Jesus' victory over the temptations of the devil therefore was evidently made possible by the Holy Spirit and that set the stage for His ministry which involved casting out devils and delivering many from spiritual bondages and afflictions.

The day of Pentecost saw the disciples of Jesus also have the Holy Spirit finally come upon them. Their meeting with the Holy Spirit had been specifically recommended with a command by the Lord Jesus himself, "And being assembled together with them, He commanded them not to depart from Jerusalem, but to wait for the Promise of the Father, 'which,' He said, 'you have heard from Me; for John truly baptized with water, but you shall be baptized with the Holy Spirit not many days from now.'" (Acts 1:4-5). Jesus explained that such a meeting would be empowering, "But **you shall receive power** when the Holy Spirit has come upon you; and you shall be witnesses to Me in Jerusalem, and in all Judea and Samaria, and to the end of the earth." (Acts 8, emphasis mine). And this is exactly what happened. The disciples practically became new people, uttering messages in languages they never had prior knowledge of and astonished all that heard and met them. As a matter of fact, their transformation was even noted by the Sanhedrin, "Now when they saw the boldness of Peter and John, and perceived that they were uneducated and untrained men, they marvelled. And they realized that they had been with Jesus." (Acts 4:13). So as Jesus promised, the Holy Spirit makes Jesus known in the believer and, unlike previous epochs, His meetings are no more rare, selective, and spotty but for all and always. God had promised to pour His Spirit on all flesh, and He did from the day of Pentecost (see Joel 2:28). Peter affirmed this when he declared on the day, "Repent, and let every one of you be baptized in the name of Jesus Christ for the remission of sins; and you shall receive the gift of the Holy Spirit." (Acts 2:38).

The Holy Spirit is the final instalment of God's plan to fellowship with His own. If He used to contact and relate with selected individuals, by the Holy Spirit He gets to make contact and remain in the lives of all who accept His gift of salvation and the grace of fellowship. By the Holy Spirit, a born-again believer can ultimately become a Christian. Thus, a Christian, who is practically Christ-like in all his ways, is so by the enabling power and presence of the Holy Spirit. This attests to the significance of a meeting with Him and the necessity of it.

Reflection

1. *Assess now*: Have you ever given a thought to the person and role of the Holy Spirit? Do you believe He is God and present now? There are many who are of the belief that the age of the Holy Spirit ended with the death of the first Apostles. Have you ever heard that, and do you concur? Has it ever crossed your mind how a person becomes born-again or comes to repentance and the new life in Christ? Would you affirm after reading this chapter that you have met the Holy Spirit as a believer, and if so, is there a prevailing effect besides conversion?

2. *Consider now*: The Holy Spirit is the Spirit of God and Jesus and is presently here in the world to carry on the work of Christ which is saving the lost. He convicts men of their sins and thus brings them to repentance. This serves as the initial introductory meeting with the Holy Spirit. The repentant believer then gets the chance to have a

comprehensive meeting which involves the Holy Spirit coming upon such a believer. This is some form of possessive act which brings the born-again believer under the completer behest of the Spirit. The condition is by wilful assent and helps with the transformation of the believer. Supernatural gifts are thereafter received from the Spirit for service, and power and grace are offered the believer to live a life unhindered by known weaknesses or frailties. Many people, during the time of Jesus, had the opportunity to meet Him directly and it is the same now through the Holy Spirit. He now makes sure that anyone anywhere gets to have a Jesus encounter in His vivid material absence. The Holy Spirit therefore makes it possible for the believer and body of believers (the Church) to live the reality of Jesus. This is why He must be met or allowed to meet with us.

Chapter 6

Meeting The Church, The People of God

The concept and image of the "people of God" has its basic fabric from Israel. God essentially picked out Israel as His people when He called out Abraham (see Exodus 6:7; Ezekiel 36:28). God chose Abraham to start a relationship with mankind once lost through disobedience and defiance. The end was a reality of a nation which began as a promise. The other part of the promise was to have a land following with "milk and honey", like a new Eden. Looked at closely, one could see a kind of restorative work by God – getting together with man again in Eden. For all intents and purposes, Israel was to be a model for divine relationship and Godly partnership. Besides its many failures, as an assembly, Israel still lives as a custodian of God's statutes, ways and heritage. This is more evident in the "new Israel" which is the Church. It is more inclusive, shepherded by the Messiah and saddled not with the law but by grace. The Church is the new model for God's relationship with humanity. It is to point to God and not be God.

A recall of the familiar episode in the garden of Eden gives this more clarity. We learn in Genesis 1 that God made mankind in His image and likeness and never an equal. The first man, Adam, was not God but like God. Unlike God, he was made and, though subject to another, he had a will. Adam's will and position was tested with the command of God not to eat from the tree of the knowledge of good and evil (see Genesis 2:16-17). His woeful failure suggested his abandon of submission. It is obvious that man was made by God to be wilfully obedient to Him whilst like Him but never Him. Simply put, man was created as God's mate, a partner to engage in fellowship but never to share His stage. Man is to be the created with God being the Creator. So, his place is in submission to the creator while showing himself as His likeness. Jesus and the Holy Spirit are never of this same score. They are God, never created or subject to Him. They are conclusively one with Him.

After man's fall or failure to hold his place in obedience, God initiated many instances to reconcile and reconnect with humanity. Though cast out, God reached out to man by picking or selecting those He found aligned to His righteous ways. By this, He picked the family of Noah and then later that of Abraham. Through Abraham, He wished to have a people who would submit to Him as the Creator and the only True God. As a people, they were to model the relationship which God sought from the beginning. To meet them was to meet those who were like God and pointed to Him. This, in the New Testament, is what we have come to know as the Church. In essence, the Church is, as Jesus described it, His bride or mate and never Himself (see Ephesians 5:23-24). Therefore, meeting the Church is meeting with those who were like God and not God. A lack of appreciation of this has invariably constituted the various queries and debates about certain actions or inactions of the Church. It must be realised that an encounter with a bride cannot necessarily be translated into a meeting with the groom. It is needful that we know the Church for what it is and definitely for what it is not.

Its Origin

As previously noted, the Church is an assembly mirrored after the assembly of Israel as a "people of God". The English word "church" is derived from the word *kuriakon* which means "belonging to the Lord," a word which happened never to have been applied to the New Testament period although it is found twice in the New Testament as an adjective applying to the Lord's Supper and the Lord's Day. Apparently, in the post-apostolic era, the Greeks used the term *kuriakon* to designate the church building[1]. The rather common translation of the word "church" in the English New Testament is the Greek word *ekklesia* (see Matthew 16:18; 18:17; Acts 2:47; 9:31; 13:1; 14:23; 15:22; 16:5; 20:17,28; Romans 16:4-5; 1 Corinthians 12:28; Ephesians 5:23-29; Colossians 1:18; Revelation 1:4,11). *Ekklesia* means "an assembly of people" and it is derived from two Greek words, *ek* meaning "out from," and *kaleo* which means "to call." The word translated as "called out from" or "the ones called out" resonates with the notion of Abraham's people being a group separated unto God just as Abraham was called out from his own. Originally, the word made reference to the legislative body of citizens of the Greek republic called from their various communities to serve their country.

Jesus used the word *ekklesia* to denominate the body He would build (see Matthew 16:18). When He did, He was tying up the meaning to the Jewish use of the word in the Greek Old Testament (3rd–2nd century BCE) where it referred to the "congregation" of Israel (see Deuteronomy 9:10, 18:16) and its reference in the Greek context to any assembly of people, whether constituted or just a mob (see Acts 19:32). In effect, the Church of Jesus is patterned after the Kingdom of Israel but with some additions and differences. Unlike Israel, the Church is not limited to a tribe or a geographical location. It is made up of all men and come under the leadership of Christ and no other person. Israel had laws and traditions for both its civic and religious life, bodily circumcision to affirm its covenant with God, and a temple which had an ark to situate God's presence. The Church has things differently. The circumcision of its people is of the heart (see Romans 2:28-29), the people's bodies are the temple of God and has only one new law of love which essentially fulfils the entire laws (see John 13:34; Romans 13:10). With the Church not having a typical structure or an elaborate set of statutes, it had to flesh out its own system of operations and traditions from the age of the apostles until now with the help of the Holy Spirit. In consequence, not all have been faultless with the New Testament Church, much like the Old Testament Israel since it is made up of people with their faults and not perfect gods. Therefore, the Church we sometimes get to meet is nothing like the Christ who made it.

The Church to Meet

When Jesus commissioned His disciples to bring the world to Him or God, it was all a reconciliatory and restorative act. Mankind was to reconnect to his maker with his sins redeemed and be nurtured in a relationship with Him. The disciples of Jesus, after the several years in His keep and tutelage, were to help all converts to learn after salvation, to walk with God not by a set of rules or laws but in love. Now given that love is best expressed, the disciples were to show off the life of Christ through their daily lives and living. They were not to be religious hypocrites, but pragmatic practitioners of their faith centred on Christ. The Church invariably should point to Christ and demonstrate His reality by being:

The Bride of Christ – "For the husband is head of the wife, as also Christ is head of the church; and He is the Saviour of the body. Therefore, just as the church is subject to Christ… Husbands, love your wives, just as Christ also loved the church and gave Himself for her, that He might sanctify and cleanse her with the washing of water by the word, that He might present her to Himself a glorious church, not having spot or wrinkle or any such thing, but that she should be holy and without blemish." (Ephesians 5:23-27). According to Apostle Paul, the Church is the bride of Christ that is being prepared for the day of the great banquet (see Revelation 19:7-9). This imagery helps to situate the Church in the relationship complex with Christ. As a bride, she is definitely not the groom but lives to take after Him. I have noticed how brides over time begin to take after the personality of their grooms even as they take their names. So, we see born-again believers or followers of Christ ending up being called Christians, like "Christ's Mrs" (see Acts 11:26). It is worth noting here that this tagging is meritorious and not gratuitous. Thus, a Christian isn't anybody who carries a Bible or claims to know Jesus or even got born-again today. A Christian is virtually a product after a process, and the Church a "work in progress" (2 Corinthians 3:18).

The Custodian of a New Covenant – "But as it is, Christ has obtained a ministry that is as much more excellent than the old as the covenant he mediates is better, since it is enacted on better promises. For if that first covenant had been faultless, there would have been no occasion to look for a second. For he finds fault with them when he says: 'Behold, the days are coming, declares the Lord, when I will establish a new covenant with the house of Israel and with the house of Judah, not like the covenant that I made with their fathers on the day when I took them by the hand to bring them out of the land of Egypt. For they did not continue in my covenant, and so I showed no concern for them, declares the Lord. For this is the covenant that I will make with the house of Israel after those days, declares the Lord: I will put my laws into their minds, and write them on their hearts, and I will be their God, and they shall be my people.'" (Hebrews 8:6-10 ESV). Israel was beheld by God as the old Church that failed to observe the tenets of the old covenant; a covenant which was cast in stone and practically far from the hearts of the people. With the new covenant comes new provisions, promises and arrangements. They are for all who will believe and accept the redemptive work of Christ fashioned after his immaculate sacrifice. Now, just as the old covenant was sealed with the shed blood of a lamb, so is the new covenant secured with the blood of Jesus. The occasion of the Last Supper is regarded as the instance when the new covenant was formally instituted, and the Church made the custodian: "And he **(Jesus)** took bread, and when he had given thanks, he broke it and gave it to them, saying, 'This is my body, which is given for you. Do this in remembrance of me.' And likewise the cup after they had eaten, saying, 'This cup that is poured out for you is the new covenant in my blood.'" (Luke 22:19-20 ESV).

The Church therefore has a salient function and place in the redemptive plan of God for humanity. It is clearly seen to carry on with a covenant that is not symbolised this time by the circumcision of the flesh but of the heart (see Romans 2:28-29). The Church is markedly a proud custodian of a new covenant with its attendant provisions and ordinances as it patiently awaits the second coming of Jesus Christ.

The Salt and Light of the World – "You are the salt of the earth; but if the salt loses its flavour, how shall it be seasoned? It is then good for nothing but to be thrown out and trampled underfoot by men. 'You are the light of the world. A city that is set on a hill cannot be hidden. Nor do they light a lamp and put it under a basket, but on a lampstand, and it gives light to all who are in the house. Let your light so shine before men, that they may see your good works and glorify your Father in heaven.'" (Matthew 5:13-16). As has been previously indicated, the first couple was to be a model of humanity made by God after His likeness and an exhibition of His relationship. That failed case caused the search for replacements which ended with the Church after Israel. This notion of modelling and exemplifying served as the basis for Jesus pointing out the Church as the salt and the light of the world. As salt, it stands to preserve the statutes and ways of God's Kingdom and lay waste to the works of evil. Made up of people of the light, the Church lives to show the world "the way" to a restored relationship with God and to His Kingdom. It is also to make bare the truth of God's word and to cast unsullied light on the wickedness of the world and the hidden secrets of darkness.

The Church cannot be a dark secret entity because that would be out of character. It cannot be barren since that would be incongruous to its nature. The Church can only be warm, welcoming, and that, which like salt, offers taste to a bland life. It is to lead the way and be seen by all to illuminate lives and subjugate all that is dark. People must always turn to it and never away from it. Again, as light, it may be hot at its core but that should only burn off evil bugs and make the cold-hearted warm.

The Ambassadors for Christ – "Now then, we are ambassadors for Christ, as though God were pleading through us: we implore you on Christ's behalf, be reconciled to God." (2 Corinthians 5:20). The familiar rendering offered by this depiction of the Church is too revealing to ignore. Ambassadors are known to represent the interests of their home state in another, securing a designated location for their activities and to register their presence. Ambassadors, functioning under agreed protocols and immunity, work to exhibit and offer the finest qualities of their state. They serve as the point of call for any enquiries about their state and affairs. In fact, an ambassador is practically the "distant president" of a nation resident in another state. The Church is made up of such ambassadors. They represent the Kingdom of God and must be seen to carry themselves as such. Christ's ambassador is no different in function and relevance from any state ambassador. The only challenge is that many never know this and so fail to present themselves as true, bona fide representatives of the Lord in the world just as Adam was to be for God.

The Academy of Christian Discipleship – "Therefore go and make disciples of all nations, baptizing them in the name of the Father and of the Son and of the Holy Spirit, and teaching them to obey everything I have commanded you. And surely I am with you always, to the very end of the age." (Matthew 28:19-20). The idea that the Church is somewhat a perfect body that harbours perfect souls is very much erroneous. It is partly an academy which helps its people know "the way" by learning from older disciples or chosen leaders. It is an academy with no graduates or alumni but just matured disciples who help new converts learn "to obey everything" the Lord commanded. The Church cannot therefore be expected to be absolutely impeccable in its ways and practice. It had no set organisational layouts or directives from the onset but has had to formulate its traditions and structures by the help of the Holy Spirit along the way. As an academy, it was commissioned to teach but then had to learn itself through numerous challenges and mishaps. So, it has made mistakes and that is a fact never to be overlooked nor a point to completely challenge its credibility as the bride or ambassador of Christ. Even the early Church had these challenges. Apostle Paul in his letter to the church in Corinth had to strongly scold the members for tolerating a reprehensible sexual act: a man sleeping with his father's wife (see 1 Corinthians 5:1). The Church will always be an academy with some failing students and non-perfect ones too. Under grace, it awaits the one who ultimately perfects and will do so at the appointed time.

The Church We Tend to Meet

There is no denying that there are huge expectations of the Church with its position and status as the bride or ambassador of Christ. A meeting with the Church is never couched in caution. Anyone going out to meet the Church hopes to meet that which speaks well of Christ, its Lord and Master, and represents what is adorable about God's kingdom. The trouble is, that is not often the case. The Church many tend to meet is hurting, disappointing and mostly confusing. Let's explore these:

A Hurting Church – The Church is perceived to be full of saints but that is certainly not the case in reality. It is, in fact, a body of diverse people at different stages of discipleship and spiritual experience. The worst instance is the presence of "wolves in sheep's clothing" in the fold (see Matthew 7:15). In effect, it is easy to find many wounded in the Church by the actions of purported members and even leaders. Some of the wounded leave to find healing and safety, never to return while others remain but keep hurting.

This makes for the "hurting Church" which goes on to hurt others. A meeting with such a church has no real good prospects and makes no good impressions. To think a meeting with such a church constitutes a meeting with the Church is inaccurate and unfortunate.

A Disappointing Church – The Church can be disappointing. As mentioned earlier, given the unreformed nature of some of the people in the Church what one expects to find in it turns out differently. The basis is the notion that, "they are not all Israel who are of Israel" (see Romans 9:6). Not all who we find in church are true converts that have wholly submitted to discipleship and seeking transformation of self, mind and character. There are those A. W. Tozer calls "honorary Christians" who are primarily there by family tradition rather than personal conviction. Not all Israel are of Israel. We have people who engage actively with the Church but have no constructive business with it. Sometimes as agents of the destructive one, they pursue and attend to a destructive agenda which the undiscerning may simply find as disappointing to happen in church. It is therefore important to reckon that a meeting with a disappointing church is not a meeting with the Anointed One. Christ is not the Church and clearly the Church is not Christ. Moreover, there are some individuals who believe they can hide under the guise of the Church to conduct their nefarious activities without drawing suspicion. One cannot obviously insist that a meeting with such is a meeting with the true bride of Christ. The Church may be disappointing, but it is people that make it so.

A Confusing Church – Many ask why there are so many forms of the Church with different traditions and, in some instances, hardlines which are never compromised? There are cases of noted differences based on doctrines, some on biblical interpretations and others, like I once heard, on the chosen carpet for the service hall which led to a split. All these can be confusing. I earlier mentioned the incident with a colleague pastor about a video clip that made rounds on social media platforms which had a pastor shaving the private parts of some of his members. Though the video turned out to be satirical, without a disclaimer or warning who could tell. Besides, the video was to highlight existing trends which begs the question, where is the place of such ills and aberrations in the Church? Of course, there are divisive elements and agents in the Church that add to the confusion. There are people who get to make public representations and impositions of private revelations and visions, and those who distort biblical truth on personal biases. Apostle Paul therefore made this appeal, "Now I urge you, brethren, note those who cause divisions and offenses, contrary to the doctrine which you learned, and avoid them. For those who are such do not serve our Lord Jesus Christ, but their own belly, and by smooth words and flattering speech deceive the hearts of the simple." (Romans 16:17-18). Here again, meeting a confusing church must not serve as a gauge for a meeting with Christ or God. The point is to meet God and not just the people of God.

Reflection

1. *Assess now*: What comes to mind when you hear of the Church? If you are in the Church now, what are your impressions? What do you hear people around you say about the Church today? Do you agree that the Church is not Christ and should be examined and assessed on its own merits without any bearing on Christ? Is the Church overrated to you? Do you still consider the Church needful besides its flaws and would you remain a member if one already? Do you have any intentions of getting others to join the community of the Church?

2. *Consider now*: God started out with the people of Israel as His chosen assembly to fulfil His sovereign plan of reconciling men to Himself and setting up a model relationship. That had its challenges because as earlier cited the people failed to establish a relationship without mediation. God was always behind a curtain with His laws on tablets or in the mouths of its teachers. Jesus is the archetype of Adam and from his pierced ribs, he raised a copy of Eve which is the Church – the bride of Christ. With the Church came a restored relationship which is not built on laws but on grace and love. This time, the Church gets to have God inhabiting individuals and not behind temple curtains or a personified ark. The Church is the new universal assembly with the new covenant which restores man's dominion and grace for eternity through Christ Jesus. As Christ's bride, she

is, however, not perfect now. There are questions raised about her conduct and hearts flurried by some of her actions. It is, however, fair to suggest that she is a "work in progress" which Apostle Paul summed up in his letter when he said, "Husbands, love your wives, just as Christ also loved the church and gave Himself for her, that He might sanctify and cleanse her with the washing of water by the word, that He might present her to Himself a glorious church, not having spot or wrinkle or any such thing, but that she should be holy and without blemish." (Ephesians 5:25-27).

Endnotes

1 Duffield, G. and Van Cleave, N. M. "The Doctrine of the Church" in *Foundations of Pentecostal Theology* (Los Angeles: L.I.F.E.,1983), 419.

Chapter 7

The Experience of Meeting God

I earlier shared the experience of a meeting with the king of the Asantes in Ghana. My intention was to pivot that for every other remarkable experience that could be had and to also point out some lessons. That experience helped me put that which I had with God in proper perspective. I figured the key character of every impactful meeting is its subjectiveness. It is good to have an encounter narrated to you but better to have it for yourself. What I said about my meeting with the king of the Ashanti kingdom might weigh in with all sorts of interpretations and representations, but it would have a distinctive appeal or effect should you have the privilege yourself. The famous Indian fable of the six blind men and their meeting with the elephant throws more light on this. According to the story, each blind man shared his concept of an elephant based on his determination of the part he touched. For instance, the one who had access to the tail presented the entire elephant as a likeness of a rope. How true and yet how false. His experience was his to have and only to be shared in context. Once out of context, a determination could only do more harm than good since it is tainted with personal distortions. This is why having a personal experience is worth more.

My aim with this book is not to share a meeting with God, Jesus, the Holy Spirit, or the Church, though I have that, but to stir an interest for one and make a case for it. I know of the difficulties that have been created with divine encounters that have been improperly shared or related; revelations interpretated through personal lenses and distorted truth shared with conviction because it was a subjective reality. There is a place and purpose to every experience and a context in which it must be dispensed.

I once met a pastor who was convinced it was a sin for a woman to wear a pair of trousers, like jeans, because that was man's clothing and contravened divine directive (see Deuteronomy 22:5). He was ready to shout this on the mountain tops until he travelled out of his country to another for the first time. He was in South Africa to minister and met a room filled with God-hungry men and women with many of them in trousers. In spite of the uncomfortable scene, he had a great meeting and never saw the need to call out the women as sinners because he found out the need for them wearing that piece of clothing. I asked him and he said he learnt it helped the women handle the cold weather. Questioned further about his conviction, he admitted he was obviously misinformed and had learnt the need to make interpretations and inferences in context. To the believer, it is common to have every word to Israel be a word directly to the Church. Little is said of context and much less is offered in relativity. As such, the scriptures with its divine truths have unfortunately been used to perpetuate certain notions and even atrocities. If God said to Joshua that, "every place that the sole of your foot will tread upon I have given you", does that essentially give any believer the entitlement to land anywhere and lay claim? (see Joshua 1:3). Well, it is definitely possible for God to minster the same words to any believer or have the faith of any believer align strongly with those words, but these very ones referenced were to Joshua and remain so.

The Church was given the commission by Jesus to share the gospel with the world and essentially introduce him to it. Like the woman Jesus met at the Samarian well (see John 4), the community of believers should bring the world to meet with Jesus as they have so graciously and thankfully met. It is never an exercise of imposition or hocus-pocus, but one for a subjective determination and conviction. Why send you a postcard of Vegas when I can give you a ticket to the place for your own appreciation? There is the need to meet God. There is the need for a personal engagement since that is possible and available. God is within reach and can be found according to Him once sought diligently and totally (see Jeremiah 29:13). The benefits and character of His meeting make it the more desirable and recommendable. I share a few here for your consideration and reflection. I submit that meeting God is:

Purposive – God never acts out of character, and conducts His matters without purpose or reason. He can practically do anything but chooses not to. His actions are set for some required results in time and always aim not to overwrite or overrule the will of humanity. Nothing stops God from revealing a sign in the skies to convince all people of His existence and reality. He has, however, made it the case that all who come to Him by His revelation, like the case of Moses at the burning bush, do so wilfully (see Exodus 3:2-4). So, it should never be taken lightly when God offers you an experience which challenges all rationality and commonality ever known to you. His meetings have personified signatures but an overarching element of mysticism and awe. God is interested in people and when He meets with them, He wants it to be about them. His primary reason for any meeting is to initiate a relationship with the one met. It is His primary reason for all His meetings: "Jesus answered and said to him, 'If anyone loves Me, he will keep My word; and My Father will love him, and We will come to him and make Our home with him.'" (John 14:23).

We can possibly guesstimate at this stage why many who ask for God to prove Himself or even show up at their whims never receive an answer. He is not a character at our disposition or some material evidence for any debate or research. He is God who loves, wants to be acknowledged and loved. Should God therefore meet with you because you asked Him or just chanced upon it, its reason must be determined and appreciated. There can only be a good reason for God to want to make His home with you.

Subjective – God's meetings, as I previously pointed out, have personal signatures. His meeting with one is never a meeting *with* all, but could be a meeting *for* all. We read in Genesis chapter 12 that God called out Abraham from his people and family, yet we see his journey practically led by his father Terah, according to the previous chapter. Genesis chapter 12 is therefore introduced with the words, "Now the Lord had said to Abram", indicating the subject of the instruction to migrate. The consequence of the family tagging along with Abraham was their settlement in Haran for over five years which was never intended in the plan. Progress could only be made after the death of Terah. Again, at a point, the nephew Lot, who carried on with Abraham into Canaan, had to leave him alone because of ongoing disputes and squabbles amongst their servants. Eventually, the one who met with God and was commissioned by God to relocate to Canaan ended up the sole executor of the plan. The point is God's meeting with anyone is personal, subjective, and should not just be corporately aligned or defined.

There have been many instances where people, upon a meeting with the Lord either by vision or dream or through a message by one of His servants, offer a generic interpretation or presentation. It must always be reckoned that, unless specifically directed or instructed, whatever God reveals, shows, or tells you is for you. What God points to you is not necessarily to us. You can't make what was customised for you mine. This matter has generated several misconceptions and created many erroneous situations in the Church. We have private revelations presented for public consumption like they were for such delivery. There is also the instance where private Christian journeys have been adopted by families. My child is not a Christian simply because I am one but should be one by choice. I only get to lead and point the way. Jacob grew up in a household where Yahweh was Lord and the God of his fathers, but at a point in his life, he chose to make him his own Lord: "Then Jacob made a vow, saying, 'If God will be with me, and keep me in this way that I am going, and give me bread to eat and clothing to put on, so that I come back to my father's house in peace, then **the Lord shall be my God.**'" (Genesis 28:20-21, emphasis mine). Hence, we tend to have the case where a disappointing church is so because we have many of its members only there based on the encounters of others and never their own. They live to represent a God or a Christ they have never met. How is that to work out?

Disruptive – A meeting with God is often disruptive. It is unsettling and perplexing. What was deemed normal and routine, suddenly gets displaced and offset by the meeting. In fact, no one ever gets to meet with God and remain the same in person and have what they once had be the same. Plans, knowledge or belief could be disrupted. Imagine finding out after a meeting with God that what you once knew was wrong, or your plans were simply out of line with His own for you. I experienced that when He met with me and commissioned me for His work. Everything changed for me even as I changed. My dream of becoming a pilot and flying people to various destinations of the world became, as my lovely wife will put it, a new reality of helping fly souls to one destination which is, Heaven. Moses met God as a human-assigned shepherd on the mountain of God one day and the next, he was on assignment as God-assigned shepherd to get Israel out of Egypt to the same mountain. Matthew left home one morning a tax-collector and returned that evening as a disciple of Jesus Christ never to return to the office (see Matthew 9:9).

Transformative – A meeting with God changes self. We see it very much on record that no one ever met Jesus without being impacted by him. He transformed infirmed people into heathy people and the religiously inclined into spiritually enlightened. Nicodemus met Jesus according to John 3 as a religious leader and left that meeting as a spiritual convert. In Mark 5, a demon-possessed man who was never approachable met with Jesus and that transformed him and even some swine that were nearby. When the news broke out in town, the townsfolk "came to Jesus, and saw the one who had been demon-possessed and had the legion, sitting and clothed and in his right mind. And they were afraid." (Mark 5:15). On the subject of conduct or actions, Apostle John made this assertion under the guise of this transformative nature of a meeting with the Lord: "Whoever abides in Him does not sin. Whoever sins has neither seen Him nor known Him." (1 John 3:6). This is what makes it difficult to reconcile the claim of someone's conversion and the preserved character and stance. Jacob met with God in the course of his internal struggles and physically got to wrestle with Him only to leave the meeting transformed with a dislocated hip (see Genesis 32:25, 31). Show me anyone who claims to have truly met God and I will show you a true change in them.

The merit of the point is clear; God transforms. An analogy to explore is the transforming effect of fire. Whatever comes into contact with this element never remains the same. It changes things compositionally. Now given that God is a consuming fire, it stands to reason that the effect of an encounter or a meeting with Him must be the same (see Hebrews 12:29). The Prophet Isaiah was alluding to this when he shared this divine prophesy, "'Come now, and let us reason together,' says the Lord, 'Though your sins are like scarlet, They shall be as white as snow; Though they are red like crimson, They shall be as wool.'" (Isaiah 1:18). We see Jesus make a town-crier and evangelist out of a religiously misguided Samarian woman with just a brief yet personal meeting. As He said to His disciples, they were and still are to be witnesses of Him since they have met Him and His Spirit, and transformed forever (see Acts 1:8).

Impressive – The impressive or notable nature of God's meetings cannot be discounted. When you meet with God it definitely makes an impression. Many years ago, I was invited to a church meeting by a pastor friend, and this was way before I got commissioned into ministry. He had a power ministry with the manifestation of signs and wonders at his meetings. At said meeting, I was fortunate to have a front row seat and an unhindered view of all that transpired in the space in front of the congregation. There was a woman at the meeting who came forwards to be prayed for that had a pregnancy which she had been carrying for close to two years. At the time, nothing showed this was the case until prayer for her began. At the touch of the pastor, she crashed to the floor and started wriggling and then became still. An anointed oil was then poured on her seemingly flat belly and then, right before my eyes, it started bulging. I admit that I literally saw her stomach grow. This carried on to a point when she appeared fully pregnant. That work of God was impressive and stayed with me. I had heard stories before then, but this left me speechless. That couldn't be staged. No one meets a God who does that and never gets impressed. I sometimes imagine the faces of the folks at the burial site of Lazarus when he got raised after four days (see John 11). Anyone who has met God must have a story to tell. That is, of course, after the speechless moment.

Reflection

1. *Assess now*: What formed your impressions about God? Are there notable instances or experiences which you would classify as divine? Do you know anyone who has claimed to have met God and what can you say of the shared experience if you think about it now? Have you ever given a thought to the popular school which rebuts divine experiences? Is there any validity to their cause? Do you have any thoughts on the supernatural?

2. *Consider now*: "So they called them and commanded them not to speak at all nor teach in the name of Jesus. But Peter and John

answered and said to them, 'Whether it is right in the sight of God to listen to you more than to God, you judge. For we cannot but speak the things which we have seen and heard.'" (Acts 4:18-20). Those were the remarkable words that featured in a statement made by the Apostles Peter and John when they made their defence in response to charges by the Sanhedrin. The words reveal the audacious elements that characterise the language and behaviour of anyone that had met God. The reality of it cannot be denied or easily corrupted. It is a subjective reality which is never compromised on popular grounds or demands. The experience of meeting God is telling and the impact evident. There are stories told that, when the Church came under grave persecutions in the Roman Empire, there were many believers who easily affirmed their faith and gallantly walked into the arenas to be mauled by lions or set alight at roadside mounted stakes. Witnesses could only explain such actions as possible with those who were thoroughly convinced of the truth and reality of what they had believed. You will possibly agree with this based on your own experience or you would when you have one. What sticks out and must be highlighted again is the fact no one ever meets God and remains the same. For those who do, checks need to be done.

Chapter 8

You Never Forget Meeting God

There are things we can't help but forget and some we just want to forget. You never climb to the peak of Mount Everest and then forget, or choose to forget, the experience in a jiffy. Hours spent on an operating table aren't going to peter out of your memory quickly. There are simply some experiences you can't forget, and that of meeting God is one. I tend to ask believers, when there is the chance, what their spiritual birthday is? We have our natural one and there is the supernatural one too. Every convert to Christianity goes through the "born-again" experience (see John 3:1-7). It is the moment an acceptance is made of the gift of salvation upon repentance from all sins and a new life in Christ is embraced. You may be scratching your head now and wondering if that is a familiar experience to you. If so, you can't certainly be born-again since no one wonders if they were ever born. Or you could be in the category of traditional Christians who were born to the Church and literally grew up within its four walls and never came to a personal conviction and conversion. In such instances, what you may know of God and Christianity will be all borrowed or even inherited. I will look more at that in the next chapter.

I do insist that one never forgets meeting God and it is never something that falls in the fold of some things we need to forget but that which we can't afford to. I can't imagine how anyone at the burial site of Lazarus on the day he was called out of the tomb could forget about such an experience. The condition of his body at the time, the display of supreme authority of Jesus or the image of Lazarus miraculously walking out of a tomb in burial wrappings, only makes for an unforgettable impression. How is experiencing

God split a sea in two, thus making it possible for over two million people to tread on bare ground, easily forgettable? That is the thing, debate or contend with an experience as much as you want but that does not take away its reality or validity from the one that experienced it.

Things We Need to Forget

There are things we need to forget. Some happenings, experiences, events, and issues that bring back some emotional pulses and effects. There is this notion touted that we must forgive and forget. It appears to have Christianity written all over it but that is not fully the case. Christians are primarily urged and even admonished to forgive since their own forgiveness from God is contingent on them forgiving others (see Matthew 6:14-15; Mark 11:25). There are about fifteen scriptural verses or references on believers' forgiveness alone. It is never the case that Christians are to forgive and forget as if that should come easily to them. They are to forgive, but forgetting is an entirely different ask. Who can just forget about a bitter experience? An acrimonious divorce, a back-stabbing friend, a failed investment due to trust or broken promises, none are forgotten easily. In fact, any true capacity to forgive and forget is only divine. It is only God who has clearly admitted to being able to forgive and forget: "I, even I, am He who blots out your transgressions for My own sake; And I will not remember your sins." (Isaiah 43:25). So, God forgives and forgets, particularly our sins, and needs to do that apparently for His own sake. I guess He doesn't need to remember our ugly past should we step before Him at any point in time for a favour. Which is equally the reason why we need to forget some things. Not forgetting affects progress.

We need to forget the very experiences which tend to break than make. Their toxicity must not be underestimated or deprecated. Any reminder is a total recall. They have serious repercussions for our mental and even physical state. I bear a testimony to this. Many years ago, I had a terrible experience with someone which had to do with some malicious allegations and lies. It was a difficult experience for myself and my family, and more so since I had no way of offering a defence. The best I could do by divine grace was to forgive and move on but that was fictive. Any time I met this individual, my heart paced, and my breathing laboured. That was not moving on. I was in trouble, festering a toxic compound of anger, hatred and injustice. It immobilises and is alarmingly unhealthy. That was when I realised I needed to forget and not just forgive. I feared I was one day going to have a heart attack if that persisted. How did I forget? I never did that by myself like many try to. To forget about difficult and damning experiences, you need help. How easy is it to be in close proximity at any point with the very same one who caused you an unforgettable pain and not remember? You need help. I got mine from the one who claims to be able to forgive sins and never remember them ever again. In fact, should you ever ask God if He remembers a certain hideous sin, His response will be, "what are you talking about?". He helped me when I asked Him. This only happened when I first realised I needed to forget and needed help to do it. It is important you know this if you are ever going to need His help: "Joseph called the name of the firstborn Manasseh. 'For,' he said, '**God has made me forget** all my hardship and all my father's house.'" (Genesis 41:51, emphasis mine). Joseph affirms the cogency of this method in forgetting as he employed it in his own case. He said God made him forget about the wrong his own brothers committed against him.

You recognise how needful it is that you forget some things. There are some experiences worth forgetting, meetings and encounters worth consigning to oblivion. As said before, it paves way for progress and accord. When I got help to forget about my difficult experience with someone, I admit I did pretty well in our last meeting. We had a good conversation for some time which was easy and unlaboured. I made progress, unbelievably wonderful progress; the very same I wish for you should you need it.

Things We Can't Afford to Forget

Clearly, there are some experiences which we can't afford to forget. There is that experience with your first job, first car or even first mortgage. No less can be said of your first love meeting. Racing heart, sudden attack of muteness as a man, sweaty palms and that strange sensation in the belly all make for memorial elements of your first love encounter. You can't afford to forget such an experience. It is a go-to when love takes an unbeaten track of sourness and difference. Such are the experiences we can't afford to forget. Their replay helps maintain their soundness and relevance even in the face of blight. We need them to appraise life fairly. They are meetings or experiences which set new paths and dispense new revelations. Meeting God is one. In fact, a meeting with God has the distinctive attributes which congeal the memory. There is the added element of God ensuring that you never forget His meeting. The awe-inducing moment, the incredible feeling and sometimes the exceptional backdrop all leave a mark. Recall the Israelites meeting with God at Mount Sinai, Moses' encounter with the burning bush, the message delivery to Mary of the birth of Jesus and you will appreciate the point.

It appears God does enough to ensure His meetings are remembered. The choice, however, remains for the other parties to remember. There is always the possibility and tendency for some people to live in denial of an impactful experience. I never get how they do that. How do you choose to forget that which is unforgettable? I know some bad experiences are worth forgetting with the help of God as mentioned earlier but how do you forget a good one and why would you? How do you forget the good benefits of a relationship? The psalmists had this to tell his soul, "Bless the Lord, O my soul, and forget not all his benefits" (Psalm 103:2). You would wonder how the soul could forget about *all the benefits* of the Lord, given the likelihood the psalmist brought it to the attention of his soul. So, a meeting with God can be forgotten but we can't afford to.

Be Careful Not to Forget

"Be careful not to forget the covenant of the Lord your God that he made with you; do not make for yourselves an idol in the form of anything the Lord your God has forbidden. For the Lord your God is a consuming fire, a jealous God." (Deuteronomy 4:23-24). Israel was to take precaution against forgetfulness, and this was an admonishing from God. In fact, they were to carefully consider the matter. There was a covenant to consider, which was instituted through memorial meetings and a physical scar or circumcision, and a reason to do so. Israel had enough to remember God as if God knew they would forget. He might have been influenced by their actions at the first meeting at Mount Sinai. The meeting had its impressive elements but essentially caused the Israelites to stay away and delegate Moses for any future meetings. At the same location and period, they reverted to idol worship as they raised a golden calf with the very same wealth secured from Egypt through the intervention of God (see Exodus 12:35-36; 32:1-6). So, one moment, Israel stood before God at Sinai with the remarkable display of heavenly pageantry and then in another, due to an apparent delay by Moses in a meeting they assigned to him, they turned their backs to God and raised this golden idol they claimed actually got them out of Egypt. How could a people forget so soon? How can one see the best and then turn to the worst?

Israel certainly had the tendency to forget which is why God gets to spell out their need not to. To help illuminate the essence and importance of His warning, He reveals to the people that He is a jealous God. You never get anyone to admit or relate the jealousy trait or disposition for nothing. When God did this, He needed His people to be carefully and seriously mindful. They just couldn't afford to forget:

> Be careful that you do not forget the Lord your God, failing to observe his commands, his laws and his decrees that I am giving you this day. Otherwise, when you eat and are satisfied, when you build fine houses and settle down, and when your herds and flocks grow large and your silver and gold increase and all you have is multiplied, then your heart will become proud and you will forget the Lord your God, who brought you out of Egypt, out of the land of slavery. (Deuteronomy 8:11-14)

The above passage has much we can relate with. I could even hazard the point that it is for all mankind. It overtly suggests the assumed disposition of man in the light of his relationship with his creator when all is well. How we soon forget about God when we seem to have little to remember Him by. Now is there such a case? Is it ever possible to have little to remember God by? Can we singularly lay claim to all in life and living without God's invaluable catering? Can anyone with faith in God assume a life without Him? It is very human to look to God for help or even with questions when challenges hit and to look to self when it is all well. Israel was warned to be careful not to forget meeting God and we all are since we can't afford to.

Reflection

1. *Assess now*: How have you carried on after a terrible experience? Have you ever seen the need to forgive let alone forget? Does the Christian admonishing to forgive as many times as possible seem unkind to you? Have you ever considered the tangible effects of unforgiveness? Are there things you need to forget? Are you having any help with that, or are you scrambling around under personal ego and effort? Have you ever considered a meeting with God not worth remembering if you have had one? Do you think you would ever forget meeting God?

2. *Consider now*: There is a lot we can't forget and much we need to remember. The psalmist leaned to this thought and said, "I will remember the deeds of the Lord; yes, I will remember your wonders of old." (Psalm 77:1 ESV). Nonetheless, there are things which for good reasons must be forgotten. We definitely can't keep harbouring pains of the past and massaging them for solace. God advises that we "forget the former things; do not dwell on the past." (Isaiah 43:18). We need to forget that which stifles growth and hinders progress. There are issues and situations which must not be given space in our prime emotional and mental estate. They tend to break and never make any good. These are memories not worth immortalising and experiences not worth replaying. Their place is in the bin tagged "never to be remembered". That said, there are some experiences and encounters which need to be remembered. We can't afford to forget about the goodness and mercies of God, just as Israel can't ever afford to forget the covenant made by God with the people through Abraham. You lose any of that and you miss everything else about them. It is worth considering therefore the need to keep in mind your

experiences with God. The remarkable elements, the inexplicable nature, the personal touch, all lend themselves to good memories and a need for remembrance. If you can't recall any experience then you may be in need of one or simply in denial. Which is it?

Chapter 9

I Know Him, I Know Him Not

You would agree to the fact there are times you truly wonder about some people you know. Some noted actions and deeds by them simply throw you off your axis. It is mostly the case that, at such times, you wonder if they are strange and unreal, or you are. There is so much we can fail to know about people and even ourselves. You might think it improbable, but you could surprise even yourself. I have been in numerous marriage counselling sessions and there is always this matter I wonder about with acrimonious marriages which I mostly ask parties: what changed? When you see a husband demonise a wife, or vice versa, you are forced to ask whether the person was a demon before the fact and act? Do people hide their identities, or do we fail to take notice? I guess we mainly take most things about people for granted, making way for the hope of a future change or opportunities for betterment with no reasonable merits. We can't claim to know what we really don't know. Seeing someone with the Bible walk out of a church building doesn't simply suggest the same is a Christian. Not all at the shopping mall are shoppers.

There are those who claim to know God yet don't and many more who tick questionnaire boxes as Christians but have not the faintest affiliation. But who is to tell until you see their deeds or ways. Besides, there are many voices who will vehemently appeal any effort to class them as unchristian because they are certain they are, in spite of the many questions they raise with their actions. Some would argue the classical point that what they do is a matter for God alone to judge. Apostle Paul would disagree: "What business is it of mine to judge those outside the church? Are you not to judge those inside? God will judge those outside. 'Expel the wicked person from among you.'" (1 Corinthians 5:12-13). So, for a Christian to question the rebuke or discipline of their peers, that signals more issues at play. Let's explore a few.

That Is Who We Are

There are many generations of Christians who simply see themselves as none other than that. They can't imagine themselves being anything else given their background and orientation. Born to Christian parents, raised in Christian homes and fostered in Christian communities, such individuals essentially consider themselves as Christians. That is who they are. They see no point in ever suggesting otherwise. In fact, some see that as wrong and even delusional if you do. No work on Sundays or Saturdays, be in church for Easter and Christmas services, know some hymns and keep a Bible; these come as mandatory expectations. Many will be quick, including myself, to view that as a good thing and clearly fitting the will of God. What is wrong with having the Lord worshipped and known in all communities? The only problem is the culturalization which ensues.

When one gets to identify with Christianity because that happens to be the community culture, either by prominence or tradition, then it makes for no subjective experience and choice. We had that happen in the Roman Empire. When Christianity became the official religion of the empire by the edict of Milan in 313 CE, it did become convenient to be a Christian. Most people became Christians not because they chose to be but because they had to be. In fact, some went to the extent of adapting some Christian ways and practices to known and familiar pagan forms. This is where we have the rampant Christianisation of anything and everything with the notion that, once that is done, it is fitting for Christianity and palpably holy. The effects are grim and corruptive, and the things done in the name of Christianity, alarming. Anything chosen to be done in tradition tends to lose individualistic perspectives and becomes a generic labelling exercise. That means, once I have a pastor as a father,

I can only be a Christian son. Labelling. We get to have the strange form of this in the unique sectarian landscape of Northern Ireland where, for instance, atheists are either considered Catholic atheists or Protestant atheists. Labelling. Go figure.

To be a Christian must, and should always, be a matter of choice. You choose to become a child of God now unlike being born one by the old Abrahamic covenant: "Yet **to all** who did receive him, to those who believed in his name, he gave **the right to become** children of God—children born not of natural descent, nor of human decision or a husband's will, but born of God." (John 1:12-13, emphasis mine). In essence, you don't become a child of God because your father or mother is one. The thing is you actually stand a better chance of becoming one by choice since you get to be exposed to godly ways and thought by your father or mother (see Acts 16:31). Knowing God or meeting Him or Jesus needs to be a personal and wilful act to ensure accountability. You need to know God for you so you can be personally accountable to Him. Thus, you are not a Christian by tradition but one by choice. It is who you choose to be.

Life in the Arena of Deceit

Jesus had a serious problem with the Pharisees of his day. He considered them religious adherents who had strong traditional inclinations. They were sticklers for the law or written code. His main problem with them was their deceitful and hypocritical nature. They never did what they asked others to do by the law. Jesus said to them, "Woe to you, teachers of the law and Pharisees, you hypocrites! You are like whitewashed tombs, which look beautiful on the outside but on the inside are full of the bones of the dead and everything unclean. In the same way, on the outside you appear to people as righteous but on the inside you are full of hypocrisy and wickedness." (Matthew 23:27-28). That is what can be said of traditional Christians today. Christianity seems, to such people, an inherited norm to be promoted but never a closely embraced reality. These folks will essentially ask you to do what they say and never what they do. Going to mass or worship services, taking communion and getting wed at the church appeal to their appropriate choices but never their valued ones. They would claim to be Christians without a moment's thought but would struggle when asked to truly live as one. Many just know how to put on the act.

I recall a lady who lived in my neighbourhood many years ago. Young then, I knew she was a Christian because she went to church every Sunday with her white headgear and her Bible held up to her chest as she carried her handbag. One day, she had a quarrel with another lady on a Sunday morning. The other lady made such a raucous which attracted many in the neighbourhood, including myself. I saw this Christian lady in the face of the assault maintain an admirable composure until she said at a point, "You will see when I return from church". And the other lady did see when she returned. After getting into a casual dress, she went looking for the other lady with all her cylinders firing. The other lady had obviously lost any fervour or interest in the quarrel after the passage of time but was forced to revive it. It was pitiful. That was when I figured out what it meant to look like a Christian and to be one.

Apostle Paul believed that, "anyone who belongs to Christ has become a new person. The old life is gone; a new life has begun!" (2 Corinthians 5:17 NLT). In effect, we see a person in Christ as one who has become and not one who was. There is a transformation and a point at which that began. An old life of sinfulness gives way to that of righteousness. The power of sin is broken by Him who never sinned (see 1 Peter 2:22; 1 John 3:5). As such, the new person in Christ finds sin as a remote interest and practically flees from it as admonished by Apostle Paul (see 2 Timothy 2:22). We can easily say from the above that any new person in Christ should be able to tell at which point he or she made the turn. If you as a Christian are still on the sinful way, the logic stands that you are not who you say you are: "Those who have been born into God's family do not make a practice of sinning, because God's life is in them. So they can't keep on sinning, because they are children of God." (1 John 3:9 NLT). Many who fail to come to terms with this find themselves in the arena of deceit where they engage with the fake and hypocritical, like the Pharisees, because they are fake themselves. These wear supposedly Christian "clothing" while committing unchristian acts. They have not truly met the "Christ".

When You Notice Wrongs and Failings

The righteous or true Christians notice failings and don't embrace them. They never call evil good and good evil (see Isaiah 5:20). They won't fail to grieve in their hearts any abuse in the Church, let alone commit them. There is nothing usual about unusual acts in Christ to them. You will never find them sleeping easy in any environment of sinful acts and inclinations. Like Lot in Sodom, they can hardly bear the stench of immorality that overwhelms their streets, so linger at the city gates away from it all (see Genesis 19:1; 2 Peter 2:7). They notice the wrong about self and others. Do they become comfortable with that? No, not when they have the Spirit of Christ. They make no excuses for wrong and make righteousness their gallant pursuit. The question is, what do you do when you notice wrong or sin?

Your response to sin offers a fair indication of your level of spirituality and place in Christianity. As a convert to Christianity, your conscience gets replaced with the Holy Spirit. So, unlike any other human with a conscience which offers a moral compass, you are directedly guided by the Holy Spirit who convicts (see John 16:8). At any point when you trespass, you can't fail to notice his conviction and urge for repentance. With Him, you can't repeat wrongs. You can never find it easy and acceptable persisting in any iniquity. Yes, it is on record that the righteous may fall but he is not to remain fallen (see Proverbs 24:16). Therefore, what we sometimes consider as moral or character failure in the Church may actually be just evidence of botched conversions. An individual who gets converted upon a true meeting with Christ cannot be saddled with sin when the Holy Spirit has taken up a seat in him. Again, yes, he may sin but never remains in it and never goes to any length to cover it. The same doesn't help others to dress up their wrongs in liberal sentiments and appellations. Apostle Paul said, "We who are strong ought to bear with the failings of the weak and not to please ourselves. Each of us should please our neighbours for their good, to build them up." (Romans 15:1-2). It is obvious there will be some weak or immature members in the Church, but Paul suggests they are to be helped out of their failings and not tolerated to remain in them. Every Christian needs to gauge the response when wrong is done or in the midst of wrong since that is an apt test of conversion and transformation.

Many will find that though they may admit that they know Christ, they actually know him not:

> "Not everyone who says to me, 'Lord, Lord,' will enter the kingdom of heaven, but only the one who does the will of my Father who is in heaven. Many will say to me on that day, 'Lord, Lord, did we not prophesy in your name and in your name drive out demons and in your name perform many miracles?' Then I will tell them plainly, 'I never knew you. Away from me, you evildoers!'" (Matthew 7:21-23)

Reflection

1. *Assess now*: Have you ever wondered about the abysmal behaviour of some Christians and tried to make sense of it? Has the question of their conversion ever been considered by you before now? What do you make of the subject of traditionalism in Christianity where connections are seemingly by heritage and hardly by choice? Do you agree one cannot be born a Christian? Have you considered before now the logic and rationale for a person redeemed from the power of sin and yet remains hopelessly bound to it?

2. *Consider now*: There is a credible presence of deception in the Church and Christianity. For centuries, the Faith has had heretics, divisive elements and imposters. From its leadership to the laity, the Church has had wolves and charlatans. Most are by choice and some by circumstance. Jesus helped us with the method of knowing them – by their fruits. As fruit inspectors, we can't claim to miss what we see. Fruits are fruits and they come from seeds. What we see people do comes from a deeper place: their heart. We need to realise that even a converted person or disciple of Christ may sin which will make it an exceptional incident and never a norm. Normalcy indicates or suggests persistence and practice. That can never be from the converted. The bane of this anomaly is the situation created by what I call botched conversions. This is where we have induced spiritual experiences based on associations or affinity. An example is having

someone born into a Christian community and growing to think he or she is one. Another is seeing a pastor's assistant or aide setting up shop as a pastor after some time with the understanding that he had learnt the ropes as if ministry is some kind of a trade. The result is the headache and heartache that are delivered with their actions. The strangest element of it all is the conviction these have and their ability to persuade others in their arena of deceit. They unfortunately lead many astray and raise questions for many every day. You might have met a few of these Christians or may be wondering if you are one yourself, but what is worth considering is what would Jesus say in a meeting one day should they or you call Him "Lord"?

Chapter 10

Blaming The Church

Jesus Christ founded the Church before His departure from Earth after His death and resurrection. He had just about a hundred and twenty disciples at the time of His leaving who He commissioned to carry on with His work of reconciling humanity with God (see Act 1:15). There was no rule book, no template to work with. All that the disciples knew about the new covenant was what Jesus taught them which was without any ancillary notes for future complexities. They were Jews all right who had served God all their lives through the Mosaic or Judaistic institution, which obviously made them clueless about having a Church let alone building one. We find them floundering from the start. For instance, when they decided to replace Judas who had betrayed Jesus and further committed suicide, they didn't choose another disciple as Jesus did, they cast lots (see Acts 1:23-26). They practically ran a lottery to pick a disciple when in the case of Jesus, He chose (see John 15:16). These were the early Church leaders.

Jesus had promised to build His Church but then was gone (see Matthew 16:18). So who was to build it? The Holy Spirit had been promised to help the disciples with remembering all things, to be a comforter and counsellor. It stands to reason that His coming in to glorify and manifest Christ was in line with His purpose of filling the vacuum Jesus' absence created. In fact, Jesus had at a point mentioned that, "On my account you will be brought before governors and kings as witnesses to them and to the Gentiles. But when they arrest you, do not worry about what to say or how to say it. At that time you will be given what to say, for it will not be you speaking, but the Spirit of your Father speaking through you." (Matthew 10:18-20).

This clearly amounted to a heads up for the disciples about the role of the Holy Spirit in the absence of Jesus. It is a case where Jesus is gone and the Holy Spirit is here. As a matter of fact, that appeared to be the plan. Jesus needed to leave to make way for the Spirit of the Father (see John 16:7). After His finished work on the cross, it had to be shared with all men all over the world. Could Jesus, if still physically present, do this together with doing good to all? He would have been swamped. The Holy Spirit who is omnipresent was needed. He came for all followers of Christ who together make the Church. He gets to build the Church for Jesus with His people.

There is, however, a problem. What happens in a situation where the Holy Spirit is not acknowledged, known or given room to operate? We have several instances in the Church today where the Holy Spirit is hardly acknowledged or even known. In fact, in the early Church, there was a case witnessed by Apostle Paul:

> While Apollos was at Corinth, Paul took the road through the interior and arrived at Ephesus. There he found some disciples and asked them, "Did you receive the Holy Spirit when you believed?" They answered, "No, we have not even heard that there is a Holy Spirit." So Paul asked, "Then what baptism did you receive?" "John's baptism," they replied. Paul said, "John's baptism was a baptism of repentance. He told the people to believe in the one coming after him, that is, in Jesus." On hearing this, they were baptized in the name of the Lord Jesus. When Paul placed his hands on them, the Holy Spirit came on them, and they spoke in tongues and prophesied. There were about twelve men in all. (Acts 19:1-7 NIV)

What we see here are twelve disciples who hadn't the slightest idea about the Spirit of the Father and Jesus who was to help build the Church. This was a cited instance which suggests the possibility of several existing. Imagine the repercussions. Today, we have similar circumstances. We have bodies of believers with differing understandings of the presence, role and reality of the Spirit of the Father in the Church. We have this affecting Church formation and function. Again, we have this generating a general discredit and disinterest for the Church. Why so?

Headless Churches

"For the husband is the head of the wife as **Christ is the head of the church**, his body, of which he is the Saviour. Now as the church submits to Christ, so also wives should submit to their husbands in everything." (Ephesians 5:23-24, emphasis mine). Apostle Paul explained that Christ Jesus is the head of the Church which goes to suggest that, in its present circumstances, the Holy Spirit gets also to be the head. This is so because the Holy Spirit stands in for Christ here and now as I have consistently pointed out. As such, the Church doesn't get to be without its partner. With His offering in the role of a head, the Church gets to receive from the Holy Spirit true spiritual leadership and vision. Of the five senses we have, four are located in the head which points to its importance and relevance. A church living and working with the Holy Spirit therefore is that which has its spiritual senses active because it has its head on. Headless churches are dysfunctional. They can't tell when things are in error or deceit parades in their circle.

The early Church surely had its head on. This made it operate in awe and reverence. An incident recorded in the Book of Acts exemplifies this. A couple chose to sell their property as others were doing but, in their case, decided to keep some of the proceeds before coming to the Church leaders. Apostle Peter, by the help of the Holy Spirit, discovered their act and inquired about it, to which the man denied it: "Then Peter said, 'Ananias, how is it that Satan has so filled your heart that **you have lied to the Holy Spirit** and have kept for yourself some of the money you received for the land? Didn't it belong to you before it was sold? And after it was sold, wasn't the money at your disposal? What made you think of doing such a thing? You have not lied just to human beings but to God.'" (Acts 5:3-4, emphasis mine). We see that Ananias' lie was not to the Church leaders but to the Church head, the Holy Spirit representing Christ. He died for his actions. The wife faced the same fate of death when she showed up later only to confirm the lie. The effect on the community was shocking: "Great fear seized the whole church and all who heard about these events." (Acts 5:11). That is a church with a head. It cannot be deceived neither is evil tolerated. You don't get to find evil committed under the noses of leaders without being discerned. Leaders miss nothing because the Holy Spirit misses nothing.

Today, with many churches giving no place and recognition to the head, evil is called good and masqueraders are allowed roles. It is sad to say that should Balaam's donkey be alive today it may find a role in some church as Prophet Donkey just because it prophesied once. No wonder there is so much discredit and dishonour now for the Church simply because some disciples have chosen to go headless.

Easy to Blame

When things go wrong in a church, the blame easily goes to all. Many may find this unfair or even cruel but the reality is more grievous. Jesus shared a parable of the leaven which enlightens us of the overwhelming effect of that substance in a portion of dough (see Mathew 13:33). The leaven may be a part of a whole but it makes the whole take after it. A member of a church may commit a singular act but at the end the repercussion may be borne by all in that church, either directly or indirectly. Joshua experienced this after their victory over Jericho and subsequent defeat to Ai: "So the Lord said to Joshua: 'Get up! Why do you lie thus on your face? **Israel has sinned**, and they have also transgressed My covenant which I commanded them. For **they have even taken some of the accursed things**, and have both stolen and deceived; and they have also put it among their own stuff.'" (Joshua 7:10-11, emphasis mine). This is what you need to make sense of the preceding statement by God. Before helping Israel with the victory over Jericho, God had warned the people not to make any possessions they find in the city their own. All should be destroyed. This the people did with the exception of an individual called Achan. So, in the above statement when God said, "Israel has sinned", He actually meant that man but he was part of the whole assembly. His sin was therefore the nation's sin in the terms of God.

The fairness or otherwise of this assertion can only be rationalised in the scope of two things: the nature and expectation of the Church or Israel in the past. By its nature, the Church is one and must be one for relevance and purpose. Apostle Paul explains this with his use of the human body where he assigns the head to Jesus and the body, with its numerous parts, to the Church (see 1 Corinthians 12:12-27). A body hurt is all (parts) hurt. All may end up in an ambulance and the hospital, and we never have any parts opting to stay back or away. Where a body goes, all the parts of it go. The Church functions as such. In this way, it gets to be the focus of every good or bad story even when involving a single member. It is simply because of its nature and can't be helped. We also have the high expectations which it attracts as reason for it being an easy victim for blame. Jesus essentially classified the Church as the salt and light of the world (see Matthew 5:13-16). It is to light the ways of others even as it lights up its own ways. Having nothing to hide, it is to expose all that is hidden. The Church is supposed to be seen to be flavouring the lives of people as the salt that it is. This clearly must be carried out with caution. Here is where the Church must acknowledge its intricate and delicate position and carry itself with integrity and decorum. Members are not to live for self but for all in the body (see 1 Corinthians 8:9). The place and work of the Holy Spirit must be seriously embraced to help with unifying and enabling the body to function right as one. After all, Jesus called out for a Church made up of followers and not denominations made up of partisans.

A Work in Progress

The Church is not yet a perfect body and must be graciously considered in that light. If you have ever been overly critical of the Church over some failings, look again at the premise. Did you lash out at the act of one whilst recognising the credible presence of some or was it a condemnation of all? Like the human body, the Church will have failing parts or foreign parts. People don't follow Jesus because they are without failings but simply because they have. The Church is an adequate home for the inadequate, a refuge for the spiritual refugee. It has flaws because the people that make it are working on their flaws with the help of the Holy Spirit. Some of its people have horrid pasts yet hopeful futures and challenging presents. There are murderers like Paul, thieves like Judas and prostitutes like Mary Magdalene. That is the Church to expect. At times, there are foreign parts which are mere alien implants. Like a boob job, these are not original parts but give false impressions which deceive easily. They sing hymns, pray and worship like the faithfuls but have no atom of faith. When such fail, it can't truly be called the failing of the Church but rather the exposition of imposters. Why blame the Church harshly for the misconduct of such foreign elements?

Then again, we consider the Church as under construction. We know this since Jesus said He "will build" His Church (see Matthew 16:18). It is not built yet. We know the Holy Spirit is helping with the work now. In essence, it can only be a messy site with signs of what is to come or realised. That is the thing I have noticed with construction sites; they can be dismal and disappointing, especially when you visit them with a computer-generated image in your head. You do that with the Church and you can be subject to the same experience. You need to look at the Church with the very eyes it looks at its future – hope and faith. Be gracious to the Church for that is what it enjoys from the Lord.

Error of Assumptions

There is this common experience of meeting someone only to be disappointed because the person failed set expectations. We can't help but be influenced by what we hear about things and people. As I mentioned earlier in chapter 1, a word like "paradise" suggests some blissful and heavenly images and notions, until the experience. Such is the error of assumptions. It is unwise, and sometimes unfair, to assume much about a thing before meeting it. You can't assume that a Christian or a church you are about to meet will definitely be wonderful, loving, kind, tolerant and even an epitome of sanctity. You need to wait for the meeting. Sometimes such expectations can impair experiences. Looking for what must be, can affect appraising what is, which happens a lot with the Church.

My daughter once said something startling to me in a conversation. She pointed to the awful pressure she, for instance, bears as a pastor's daughter. I had no clue of the extent of it until she mentioned it. She referred to them as "unspoken expectations". Things people expected her to be doing and not doing. Unspoken expectations. They were nagging and distressful. Like I said, I was startled. No one bothers to know her own convictions, challenges or stories, everything is assumed. Pastor's wives are no different. They are to help with everyone else's pain and never have their own. Anyone can choose not to be part of the Church but they presumably can't. They can never be found struggling in faith. That to some is pure sacrilege. The notion held is that what you assume about them is what you must find about them. Is that impartial? The thing is, all experiences are relative. If you want to see me as kind, would that be similar to my definition and exercise of kindness? Your notion of loving may be impractical in my context, but then I still love. Wouldn't you need to hear, at some point, the personal stories and views of the pastor and family before making judgements or apportioning blame? Is the Church any less? If you assume the Church to be something it is not, wouldn't it be fair to defer blame until an explanation? Don't you think it would be appropriate to leap as the Church does before making a judgement of its strength or weakness? The Church has been blamed for many things because many things have been assumed about it.

Look Unto Christ

Many people have been dissuaded from desiring a meeting with God just because of the actions and conduct of some members of the Church. It is true the Church is one body yet the presence and singularity of its constituent parts cannot be denied. The act of one is definitely not the act of all. We need to see things in their true perspective with regards to accountability (see Ezekiel 18). The Church can't be totally laden with the failings of a few. As a larger body, it points to greater grace and virtue. It points to Christ. The Church is never about itself and never should be. It is about Christ, its Lord. Anytime we have the Church make itself the centrepiece we see its failings and imperfections but when Christ is at the centre, all we see is the Perfect One and the undeniable Redeemer. So, we have the Hebrew writer encourage us to look "unto Jesus, the author and finisher of our faith, who for the joy that was set before Him endured the cross, despising the shame, and has sat down at the right hand of the throne of God." (Hebrews 12:2).

The essence of meeting the Church is not to meet the people of God but the God of the people. The people may disappoint but God won't. The people may have some imperfections but God doesn't. If God isn't driving you out of a church, then no one should. There is a story of a lady who nearly fell foul to this. She went to meet the pastor of the church she had been attending to announce her departure due to the observed conduct amongst its members. She cited gossiping, lying, backbiting and infighting as some of the appalling acts. Her meeting with the pastor was after a Sunday service which was to be her last. Noticing her resolve, the pastor asked she do one thing before she left which she agreed. He gave her a glass of water and asked her to go to the main hall of the church which still had some members chitchatting. She was to walk round the hall three times making sure she never spilled the water in the glass. After a couple of minutes, she returned carefully clutching the glass of water with her eyes glued to it. The pastor asked if she spilled any, to which replied, "Of course not, pastor." Asked how that was the case, the lady explained she kept her eyes on the glass and avoided any distractions. The pastor then asked if she noticed any of the people in the hall and some of the things they were doing, to which she replied, "No." She suddenly realised the lesson of the exercise. Once you keep your eyes on the Christ of the Church, you hardly get deterred by the acts of its members. You could have enough to blame the Church for but could you say the same about Christ or God? Always look to Christ!

Reflection

1. *Assess now*: You might have heard unpleasant stories about the Church, the question is what did you make of them? Have you ever held any assumptions about the Church and Christians? Are you of the opinion that the Church as a whole must be responsible for the pitfalls of a few? Have you considered the Church as a body with elements which are subject to failure? What have you sought to see anytime you have had the opportunity to look in the direction of the Church; Christ the head or the Church body? Do you think your view was distorted before?
2. *Consider now*: The Church has had many failings before and still does now. As a work in progress, it certainly gets overwhelmed and burdened with expectations. That wouldn't have been a problem had

the Holy Spirit received absolute control and guardianship of the Church. As a body with many parts, the Church struggles in many instances without God's Spirit. It has foreign elements which go unnoticed that cause gruesome havoc besides the numerous parties "working out their salvation" (see Philippians 2:12). Anyone would have much to blame the Church for but a closer look suggests a fairer apportioning of blame. There are the Achans who will stir up corporate predicaments but should be identified and separately addressed. Their errors and failings must not be a measure of the character and stance of all in the Church, neither should it serve as a deterrent for future discipleship. It is needful and advisable to be part of a suitable body of Christ, with suitability being determined by agent of conversion (the church which brough you to Christ), agreeable beliefs and vision. The scriptures point that, "Can two people walk together without agreeing on the direction?" (Amos 3:3 NLT). Being part of a body where you fail to integrate and be comfortable can cause many misgivings and apprehension. You get distracted from the Christ you serve to the church you serve in. Avoid that. There is the need for all in the Church, and those coming in, to keep their eyes on Jesus. He alone set out to draw all men to Himself on the cross (see John 12:32). No one else deserves the attention due Him. A distraction from Him is an attraction to others. If you should look His way always, you would have less of the Church to blame.

Chapter 11

Come Meet the Lord

There is an absolute need to meet the Lord to be clear about His existence, love and grace. It must be said that there is nothing like a personal encounter. As I recounted in chapter 2, my meeting with a king offered me an experience I couldn't dare compare to any heard stories or tales. Preconceptions, assumptions and even prejudices get sanitized by the vivid reality of an encounter. What you hear about people or things finds perspective when you meet them. It is like painting on your very own canvas with your own brush. The experience is yours to tell and for others to believe. I have heard stories about people and my meetings with them haven't mostly helped such stories. Besides, your experience with someone or something in winter may not be my experience with the same in summer. This is why it is unfair and partly misguided to, like we say, judge a book by its cover. You can't seriously use Sunday School clippings and stories to draw your final picture of God. You need to meet Him and we get to do this now through Jesus: "Jesus said to him, 'I am the way, the truth, and the life. No one comes to the Father except through Me.'" (John 14:6). This must be clarified.

It is obvious that Abraham and even his descendants never had the circumstance and reason to meet God through Jesus. They met God and had a direct relationship but under several conditions, one being faith. Then the people of Israel had their meetings and relationship with God, centred around His covenant laws and statutes. This means when you did what God had asked to be done then you were good with Him and were a friend. The challenge was to do what He had asked to be done. They were numerous, burdensome and exacting. The blood sacrifices, the civil and ceremonial laws, which formed part of the known six hundred and thirteen commandments, could all be overwhelming. Apostle Peter in the first Church Council meeting held in Jerusalem asked, "why do you test God by putting a yoke on the neck of the disciples which neither our fathers nor we were able to bear?" (Acts 15:10). So, to know God in essence came with a yoke then. What we have now is just by grace. You don't need to be born a Jew or get to live by every known command to be a friend or a child of God. You simply believe in Jesus and all that He ended up doing here on Earth for humanity and you get to have a friend in heaven. How is this so? Jesus explained that, "He who believes in Me, believes not in Me but in Him who sent Me. And he who sees Me sees Him who sent Me." (John 12:44-45). In effect, we get to believe or connect with God once we believe in Jesus, and we meet God when we meet Jesus. Don't feint an understanding of this when you don't because Jesus' own disciples had a problem grasping it:

> Philip said to Him, "Lord, show us the Father, and it is sufficient for us." Jesus said to him, "Have I been with you so long, and yet you have not known Me, Philip? **He who has seen Me has seen the Father**; so how can you say, 'Show us the Father'? Do you not believe that I am in the Father, and the Father in Me? The words that I speak to you I do not speak on My own authority; but the Father who dwells in Me does the works. Believe Me that I am in the Father and the Father in Me, or else believe Me for the sake of the works themselves." (John 14:8-11, emphasis mine)

God Amongst Men

Imagine sitting before Jesus, whose siblings, mother and family home you happen to know and He is telling you He is God in the flesh. Jesus, the carpenter's son, God in the flesh. Consider that for a moment. You wouldn't be surprised then by the doubts many held about Him and why some considered Him blasphemous and even deluded. He needed to help His case which He did with the works He performed. Only God could do what He did (see John 3:2) and He occasionally pointed that out as in the case of Philip. For Jesus to be God, it only had to be believed. His works were not completely uncommon to the people then, though a few were, and so was the consistency and rampancy. There was also the question of why God had come to live amongst men?

God had said for many centuries through His prophets that His very own shall come to live amongst His people. He was to be their Saviour and, in fact, the redeemer of all humanity. Besides, He needed to displace the myth which had developed between humanity and divinity since the fall of man. For instance, when He said, "Come now, and let us reason together … Though your sins are like scarlet, They shall be as white as snow; Though they are red like crimson, They shall be as wool." (Isaiah 1:18), how was that to be done practically? God had to be within reach and reason for a conversation. God had to be reachable to be affable. He needed to step down from the mountain to engage with His people in the valleys. His intentions and plans where well-knitted into the numerous messages of the prophets. The people heard them all right but couldn't figure out a visitation by God Himself. Yes, a Messiah was coming but to the people that surely wasn't going to be the Almighty Himself. Or was it? Consider this prophesy from Isaiah carefully and note my highlights:

> For unto us a Child is born, Unto us **a Son is given**; And the government will be upon His shoulder. And His name will be called Wonderful, Counselor, **Mighty God, Everlasting Father**, Prince of Peace. Of the increase of His government and peace There will be no end, Upon the throne of David and over His kingdom, To order it and establish it with judgment and justice From that time forward, **even forever**. The zeal of the Lord of hosts will perform this. (Isaiah 9:6-7, emphasis mine)

We find, according to the prophet, a child that shall be born to a parent but the same had been given to the world as a Son (see John 3:16). The same known as the Messiah or Christ ("the Anointed One" in Greek) shall be the Mighty God and the Everlasting Father whose reign shall be forevermore. This can only be an eternal being and if the description, together with many others, points to Jesus then He can be none other than the Mighty

God. Always revert to your own case of having a body with a spirit and soul anytime you are trying to make sense of the divine arrangement and nature of the Trinity.

Come Meet Jesus

Jesus is simply God as a person we can relate to. He is the one we can meet to reason with, according to Isaiah. He did this with Abraham on the subject of Sodom and Gomorrah's destruction (see Genesis 18:22-33). That has always been His preferred way, fellowshipping with His people in the reality of His grace and love. Adam and Eve heard His footsteps and we get to hear that again through Jesus. The Hebrew writer referred to Him as our sympathetic High Priest: "Seeing then that we have a great High Priest who has passed through the heavens, Jesus the Son of God, let us hold fast our confession. For we do not have a High Priest who cannot sympathize with our weaknesses, but was in all points tempted as we are, yet without sin." (Hebrews 4:14-15). So, an invitation to meet Jesus is a direct invitation to meet God. If you believe Him to be who He is and not a carpenter's son or some Galilean who had a remarkable life, then you are on course for a meeting. His meetings could be God-driven or man-driven.

God-Driven Meetings

God-driven meetings are initiated or arranged by Himself. These are meetings which may catch anyone by surprise. They are primarily centred on God's purposive will and intent for those involved. We see an example in the meeting of Moses at the burning bush and that of Abraham at Mamre (see Genesis 18:1). A meeting of such nature is mainly under God's own behest and interest. He simply steps before you and waits for you to invite Him in or approach Him. He, however, does well to draw your attention in most cases since He desires the meeting. The Old Testament is awash with such remarkable and often startling encounters. Invariably, parties to such meetings end up doing something for God or handling His business. Some call it a "divine calling". It is a known precursor to commissions and ministries. Here, you have God approach you mostly out of the blue either personally or through an angel for a chat (see Gideon in Judges 6:11-24). The reason why we say that they involve commissions is that the chats often end with a divine assignment.

We have the case of the twelve disciples in the New Testament. None aligned themselves or joined his fold by a personal request or application but by Jesus' calling or choice. He said to them, "You did not choose Me, but I chose you and appointed you that you should go and bear fruit, and that your fruit should remain, that whatever you ask the Father in My name He may give you." (John 15:16). We here again see the commissioning factor. Apostle Paul spoke of his own meeting when he said, "Then last of all He was seen by me also, as by one born out of due time. For I am the least of the apostles, who am not worthy to be called an apostle, because I persecuted the church of God." (1 Corinthians 15:8-9). This meeting happened in the course of Paul's journey to Damascus (see Acts 9). An inherit character of these meetings is the same: unsolicited or spontaneous. It conforms to the disruptive nature of divine meetings cited earlier. They are sudden, uncontrolled and undeniable. It is the case where God takes an interest in you and so appears to you. Not all may have such a unique and singular encounter, which makes it a thing of honour. Yes, you could be tempted to look at the fairness of it all but focus on the honour. This means when you get to meet with God in any means He chooses, it should be regarded as priceless and fortunate. It mustn't be taken lightly or scorned, neither must that of anyone who claims one be derided. You need to realise that meeting God now would practically be a meeting with His Spirit which is also the Spirit of Jesus. As such, the meeting will be devoid of any physicality. I am sorry but you are not going to have Jesus walk up to you at some point, neither are you going to have an angel appear suddenly with a proclamation or message from God. It is hardly the case now. Meetings today are in mainly unconventional ways and definitely never the same with everyone. Paul heard the voice of Jesus, yours could be a sudden stirring in the heart, a knowing or a profound dream or vision. What, however, lingers as proof is the conviction you have about your need for God, a birth of faith, and a sudden sense of realisation of the spiritual or the supernatural. Special then takes on a new meaning for you. You are not special to meet God but you are special because He met you.

Man-Driven Meetings

There are man-driven meetings with God. In fact, God calls for them. These are His words through the Prophet Isaiah, "'Come now, and let us reason together,' Says the Lord." (Isaiah 1:18a). We see that God is not hiding and very much interested in a meeting. He is there to be found and near to be reached. Isaiah further suggests that, "Seek the Lord while He may be found, call upon Him while He is near." (Isaiah 55:6). Man-driven meetings require the effort and interest of any person involved. It is essentially man looking to meet with God or agreeing to meet up as the Lord knocks on the hearts of men (see Revelation 3:20). You may really wonder what will make a meeting with God possible? Here are a few pointers:

Seek with the Heart – "And you will seek Me and find Me, when you search for Me with all your heart." (Jeremiah 29:13). God wants to be sought after with the heart, and all of it. It is never an exercise of the intellect or mind but just the heart. This explains why many who have tried to reason God out have mostly failed. You don't get to figure God out like a thing under a microscopic lens because He is not. A heart that seeks God does so not as a feat to prove notions and theories but to find a Father and Lord. It is typically a spiritual exercise and not a scientific one. The heart with which you seek Him must be pure: "Blessed are the pure in heart, For they shall see God." (Matthew 5:8). Your heart can't be tainted with worldly inclinations, influenced by personal ambitions or sold out to a quest. It must be like that of a lost child looking for the father, a crying baby seeking the comfort of the mother's bosom, a zealous researcher looking for a long-lost treasure or a lover's search for the missing partner.

King David was said to be a man after God's own heart (see 1 Samuel 13:14). I believe the expression has a figurative and a literal meaning. Figuratively, it points to the fact David was God's notable choice since he aligned himself with God's ways and will. The literal meaning, however, suggests a finding by David which made him relate with God in a way none of his peers did. He simply went "after God's heart" which offers the picture of a kid running after an ice cream truck in a neighbourhood. He obviously did this with his own heart and in the safety of his belief. This is reflected in the Psalm 42: "As the deer pants for water, so I long for you, O God." (Psalm 42:1 TLB). A heart that seeks God first believes that He exists just like the deer believes in the existence of streams. As such, a search is never without hope nor is it a desire without prospects. If you aim to meet God, make sure you make it a heart-work and never a mind-work.

Seek with a Broken Heart – "My [only] sacrifice [acceptable] to God is a broken spirit; A broken and contrite heart [broken with sorrow for sin, thoroughly penitent], such, O God, You will not despise." (Psalm 51:17 AMP). God will never ignore anyone who seeks Him with a broken heart; a heart which considers itself unworthy to approach His glorious presence and perfect light. Scriptures show numerous instances where people who met God could do nothing but bow or prostrate before Him. A heart that seeks Him can only do likewise, bow and be torn to bits by the sense of unworthiness and imperfection. It can be said that the proud never find God, they happen to be found by Him by His will and grace. If you seek God with a sense of entitlement or arrogance, then you may search for a long time. Loftiness doesn't find God but finds that which appears as an angel of light, the devil. God can't be found because you want to find Him but can be found because you love to find Him. So, it is right to seek God with the heart but as we can see it should be with a broken heart: "The Lord is close to the broken-hearted…" (Psalm 34:18 NIV).

Seek with Your Whole Heart – "If you look for me wholeheartedly, you will find me." (Jeremiah 29:13 NLT). God is to be sought with the whole heart which appears to be the way He wants things to be done with Him. Being a jealous God, He seeks devotion and exclusivity (see Exodus 34:14). For instance, we see our love for Him urged to be "with all your heart, with all your soul, and with all your strength." (Deuteronomy 6:5). This suggests diligence and commitment with the things of God. No one can tell how many times you will have to knock on the doors of Heaven for access. You may be heard the first time but the moment of a granted meeting is unpredictable. This is where and why you will need your whole heart in the exercise. Perseverance and fervency must critically feature. You must be determined to meet God. If "you will seek the Lord your God… you will find Him if you seek Him with all your heart and with all your soul." (Deuteronomy 4:29).

An Open Invitation

God calls all to Him. There is no selection process or need for an appointment. The scriptures indicate that, "**as many as** received Him, to them He gave the right to become children of God, to those who believe in His name: who were born, not of blood, nor of the will of the flesh, nor of the will of man, but of God." (John 1:12-13, emphasis mine). Many have the opportunity to be part of God's family as we can see from this scripture. It is no more the exclusive privilege of the descendants of Jacob. All can join now, not by natural birth, but by God's spiritual birth which comes through a belief in Christ. Believe in Him to meet Him. Like I said before, there is no selection process to meeting God but just a simple, singular condition – believe. This action word involves a personal effort which is not weighted down by assumptions, man-made theories or prejudices. It is of a pure heart after a pure God. That is the condition.

Jesus once said, "Come to Me, **all** you who labour and are heavy laden, and I will give you rest." (Matthew 11:28, emphasis mine). Here again, we find the open invitation. God is clearly not keeping Himself away anymore behind curtains, as was the case in the Jerusalem Temple. He is approachable and reachable having purposefully and symbolically ripped the curtains off the Jerusalem Temple (see Matthew 27:51). The privilege of meeting Him is no more the right of a few but a benefit to all. We have warning though that reaches us from an old prophet: "Seek the Lord while He may be found, Call upon Him while He is near." (Isaiah 55:6). What the Prophet Isaiah makes known to us is the limitedness of the opportunity or privilege we have in meeting or seeking God. It is here now but certainly not forever.

Now, let's take a moment to explore your circumstance. You might have read this book to this point because it is well within your choice of reading materials or it just addresses a Christian subject. You might have read this far because it illuminates the subject of meeting God though not exhaustively, as if that can ever be done. What remains, and of interest to me, is whether you have been helped to determine if you have ever met God or Jesus. Can you say you are a Christian after having had a convincing experience with the Lord? Or do you fall within the category, like me, of those who were born into the community of the Church and practically grew up as Christians? Would you want to meet God? Would you love to stay in His presence? Let these questions linger so they find their way into your heart. They might stir up an interest or steer you to a place of a meeting. Remember though that God is nearer than ever before through Jesus and waiting for your call.

Reflection

1. *Assess now*: Before now, did you consider yourself an outlier to the knowledge and experience of God? Would you call yourself a traditional Christian or a born-again one? Were you ignorant of the difference before now? Have you ever felt meeting God was overrated and improbable? Have you ever had any deterrents? Would you consider meeting God now? Are you clear about His open invitation?

2. *Consider now*: There was a time, when not reaching all men, God reached out to a few who were willing and faithful enough to walk with Him. All the while, He planned a wider outreach. We had one of His prophets hint at this: "And it shall come to pass afterward That I will pour out My Spirit **on all flesh**; Your sons and your daughters shall prophesy, Your old men shall dream dreams, Your young men shall see visions. And also on My menservants and on My maidservants I will pour out My Spirit in those days." (Joel 2:28-29, emphasis mine). This is unlike God and never in His known way of working, but, in this prophesy, He promises to have His Spirit dwell with anyone who will allow or receive Him. It is like having many Davids and Samsons all over the place; kings, priests and prophets in every corner and arena. God wants to meet all men and be part of their lives. He needs no one wandering around with questions when He is around to answer them. He wants to be met and known and

thus remarkably and intentionally gave all access to His Temple Holy of Holies. You have God within reach, Jesus to relate with, and no excuse to remain in the dark. For an open invitation that has been offered, what is required is an earnest and timely response. You would agree that nothing stays open endlessly. In fact, you wouldn't have your personal doors in a such state. All are invited for a meeting and a relationship and the take-up time is now!

Chapter 12

Set Others Up

"The woman then left her waterpot, went her way into the city, and said to the men, 'Come, see a Man who told me all things that I ever did. Could this be the Christ?' Then they went out of the city and came to Him." (John 4:28-30). Here we have John recount an event that transpired in a city of Samaria. You may be familiar with the story since I mentioned it in chapter 4. Jesus meets a lady from the city and gets to chat with her. At the end of the encounter, she is so impressed and impacted by the meeting that she runs to town to tell all she can find. This is typical of Jesus encounters. You just want to tell, which is what I am doing. I used to have this image when young about the need and essence of telling others about Jesus or God. I figured that should anyone find themselves together with others on a journey through a desert or arid place with a terribly dry throat and chanced upon a spring of water, I don't think the sane and even moral thing to do would be to keep that discovery from others. That is, you have your fill of such priceless refreshment and walk away whilst looking on as others stagger, hopeless and dreary. Could you live with that? Can you ignore a fallen sign which warns drivers of a damaged bridge when you can put it up again? That is what it means for not setting others up for a similar meeting you have had with God. If you have had a meeting, help others too.

Can't Be Silenced

Jesus tried on many occasions to silence people he had helped after meeting with them:

Now a leper came to Him, imploring Him, kneeling down to Him and saying to Him, "If You are willing, You can make me clean." Then Jesus, moved with compassion, stretched out His hand and touched him, and said to him, "I am willing; be cleansed." As soon as He had spoken, immediately the leprosy left him, and he was cleansed. And **He strictly warned him** and sent him away at once, and said to him, "See that you **say nothing to anyone**; but go your way, show yourself to the priest, and offer for your cleansing those things which Moses commanded, as a testimony to them." However, he went out and began to proclaim it freely, and to spread the matter, so that Jesus could no longer openly enter the city, but was outside in deserted places; and they came to Him from every direction. (Mark 1:40-45, emphasis mine)

Mark seems to be making a point in writing about the above incident the way he did. He certainly wasn't pointing out the error of a man but the ineffectiveness of an order. It is a case where a man dared to disobey Jesus and it seemed all right. A leper was warned not to speak about Jesus or whatever he did for him and he did the opposite. He couldn't be silenced. There was no way he could keep quiet about his deliverance from what once kept him away from people. I am sure that is what made the order inept. This man for years had stayed away from people because of his ailment (see Leviticus 13:45-46). Suddenly, he appeared healthy after meeting Jesus and then sent to present himself before the High Priest, as the law required, to affirm his healing. He sure wasn't going to make his way through empty streets or alleys or meet people who wouldn't recognise him. That couldn't be. He sure would have had lots of explaining to do. He had to tell the story behind his sudden stroll through the streets amidst the crowd and I am sure he loved telling it.

Here is another incident. Jesus once met two blind men: "And when He had come into the house, the blind men came to Him. And Jesus said to them, 'Do you believe that I am able to do this?' They said to Him, 'Yes, Lord.' Then He touched their eyes, saying, 'According to your faith let it be to you.' And their eyes were opened. And Jesus sternly warned them, saying, '**See that no one knows it.**' But when they had departed, **they spread the**

news about Him in all that country." (Matthew 9:28-31, emphasis mine). You could ask the question that if the order not to speak about him wasn't often obeyed, why did Jesus keep giving it? Was it some form of a test? Did those who disobey fail or actually pass? What would you have done in such circumstances? Some say it is better to apologise for doing a thing worth doing when asked not to. In ministry, I have seen people not saying a word about what God has done for them. What must we make of that? Would you rather keep silent about your experience with the Lord or sound it from the rooftops?

There Is Much to Be Experienced

If you take the time to follow the exploits of NASA, the American Space Agency, you would be elated with the advances made in space exploration and amazed with what they keep finding. A lot of the work that is being done now is in concert with agencies of other countries. In fact, there is much being done rapidly and efficiently in that manner. Imagine if NASA practically sabotaged the efforts of other nations or entities in their space ventures, what good would that do for them and all men? There is much of space out there to be ventured and explored. There is much more experience to be had. No one can claim to know or have experienced all about space let alone God who created it all. So, there is definitely much to be experienced and shared. What matters though is the acknowledgement or recognition. We can't have billions of the inhabitants of the earth and many more in the grave wrong or deluded about their experiences with God. They simply can't all be wrong. God exists and Jesus walked the earth to confirm that. If it is hard to imagine God then look in the way of Jesus. This must be acknowledged. Jesus is God that tasted our bread, had our thirst and suffered our afflictions. He acted as no superman because no superman walks on the streets every day. He lived like an average man so all men could relate to Him. That was God giving us no excuse not to reach out to Him.

Many may not believe in Him but He believes in all. How troubling that may be to God. He is regarded as unreachable, yet when He makes Himself tangible and within reach, He is reckoned as false and an imposter.

For some who really want to see God to believe, how would they want to see Him? I am sure seeing Him in the fullness of His glory won't do since none can survive that. So, they will have to settle for Jesus. Believing in Him sets up a meeting with God and there is much to be experienced without any preconceptions. NASA believes there is much out there in space to be explored and equally there is much to experience about God if anyone would believe that He is closer than the next breath.

Stop No One

We need not stop anyone from believing in God or seeking Him. Just as we have distinctive bodily features so do we tend to have distinctive experiences. I have learnt to engage with people on this principle. I am not guaranteed a similar experience you had with someone. The fact that you experienced no kindness with someone doesn't mean that I may not. I only need not be preoccupied with your experience so I can experience my very own. Like the blind men's experience with the elephant, all need to have their experience of God. Jesus felt that the Pharisees in His day were guilty of this: "But woe to you, scribes and Pharisees, hypocrites! For you shut up the kingdom of heaven against men; for you neither go in yourselves, nor do you allow those who are entering to go in." (Matthew 23:13). This is what really happens to those who fail to experience God. They miss His overwhelming light which exposes all intentions and inclinations making them bare before self. That alone sanitises and sanctifies motives and views making one better and never bitter. At the end, God's love impacts who He encounters and is carried on to others. I have therefore come to know that many who speak bitterly about God and even challenge His existence have more to tell than they say. Some came to that conclusion because He never showed up in a way they wanted or possibly never answered at the time they called. Yes, that may be their reality that cannot be decried but that shouldn't cause them to keep others from their own experience. God is there to be met not at our whims but out of the genuineness of our whole heart. If you never get God to do things your way then you may need to learn to do things His way.

There are instances too where we get to be overprotective. The disciples of Jesus fell into this error and nearly drove away some children from Him: "Then little children were brought to Him that He might put His hands on them and pray, but the disciples rebuked them. But Jesus said, 'Let the little children come to Me, and do not forbid them; for of such is the kingdom of heaven.'" (Matthew 19:13-14). Maybe the disciples didn't want Jesus to be bothered but they never heard Him complaining. No one can ever be seen to be bothering God. He doesn't need us protecting Him, His Image or Name. The last time someone tried to supposedly keep Him from falling, he got killed (see 2 Samuel 6:7). We shouldn't stop anyone from God or the search for Him. He deals with us according to our personal level of faith and so if we have someone crazy about Him then that should be respected. If you are not then that is also fine. There was an astute Pharisee called Gamaliel who in the early days of the Church had this to say to the elders of the people at the time:

> "Men of Israel, take heed to yourselves what you intend to do regarding these men. For some time ago Theudas rose up, claiming to be somebody. A number of men, about four hundred, joined him. He was slain, and all who obeyed him were scattered and came to nothing. After this man, Judas of Galilee rose up in the days of the census, and drew away many people after him. He also perished, and all who obeyed him were dispersed. And now I say to you, keep away from these men and let them alone; for if this plan or this work is of men, it will come to nothing; but if it is of God, you cannot overthrow it—lest you even be found to fight against God." (Acts 5:35-39)

He was so right. The movement of Jesus lives on until today and is still unstoppable. I conclude my writing on this basis and truth. If God exists and is there to be met, then I need not cajole you. If His Son and Church lives on then your meeting will come on if only you *believe*!

Reflection

1. *Consider now*: Many still struggle with the reality of spirituality. It is either a lie or a mystery but hardly a truth for so many. The trouble

is reconciling the existence of God in the midst of wanton wickedness in the world. How can there be a good God overseeing all, that is the question. The simplest conclusion for some then is either He doesn't exist or never cares for humanity. So there is either no God to meet and if there is, would it be worth meeting given His indifference? God however addressed all these questions when He joined our kind by birth. Born of a woman He suckled and knuckled like everyone else in this life. He answered questions and addressed concerns from the age of twelve (see Luke 2:42-47). When He walked the streets, the sick received healing from Him and the destitute had hope and joy. This is not like a God who supposedly never cares. He cared and loved to the point of finally granting freedom and life to all men through His own death (see John 3:16). God did all this so we can live less of the troubles and hopelessness we have. We only have to believe. We need to believe He exists and did show up through Jesus to be the Father, friend and Lord we have always desired. He can't be seen as unconcerned and disinterested in our plight when He is the very one asking us to "Come now, and let us reason together" (see Isaiah 1:18). In fact, Apostle Peter offers us another perspective when he said, "The Lord is not slack concerning His promise, as some count slackness, but is longsuffering toward us, not willing that any should perish but that all should come to repentance." (1 Peter 3:9).

God wants the best for us (see Jeremiah 29:11). He knows how different we are from each other and therefore regards personal meetings as the way to addressing our unique challenges and needs. So, God wants to meet with you if you will let Him. But the point is, how can you meet someone you don't believe in? This is why you need to believe in Him first and with a sincere heart, seek a personal meeting. God is best being your God so you can withstand the worse with Him. Consider meeting God now and if you have been a "church person" without a personal conviction and encounter, then ask for a meeting now. Remember, He will "stand at the door and knock. If anyone hears My voice and opens the door, I will come in to him and dine with him, and he with Me." (Revelation 3:20).

Say this: "Lord I want to meet you!"

Acknowledgements

I would like to give thanks to my wife, Vida; my children, Tracy and Lisa; and the members of my local church, the New Life International Ministry in Dublin. Thank you for your love, support and kindness.